Before
You Marry
...*Again*

Before
You Marry
...Again

DR. I. RALPH HYATT

Random House New York

Library of Congress Cataloging in Publication Data

Hyatt, Ralph.
Before you marry . . . again.

1.   Marriage.   2.   Mate—Selection.   3.   Remarriage.
I.   Title.
HQ734.H96   301.42′7   77-6005
ISBN 0-394-41247-8

Manufactured in the United States of America

2 4 6 8 9 7 5 3

FIRST EDITION

To
Susan
Glenn and Sherry
A loving family who have supported
my needs to be and to become

Foreword

As a clinical psychologist with twenty-five years' experience in counseling people before, during and after separation or divorce, I have been struck again and again by the tendency of my clients to repeat patterns when it came to falling in love or marrying—the first, the second and even the third time.

In 1976 there were over one million divorces in the United States, an all-time-high figure to that date, in a trend that seems to be constantly increasing. We also know from statistics that nine out of ten of those who divorce will marry again.

Tragically, many of these people will find that they have married the same kind of person they left behind. They will also tend to repeat the same destructive behavior with their new partners that caused them problems in their last relationship.

In order to help my clients stop repeating these destructive patterns, I gradually evolved a technique I call UNRAVELING. This method involves a *quiz* to determine my clients' basic behavior patterns, a series of questions regarding their childhood, their marriage(s) and their present needs; various *exercises* designed to lead to change; and a set of *guidelines* to help them determine what they want or need to make a happier future.

I realized that with the help of these materials and with the case histories which my clients have given me their permission to use as examples and signposts, much of the work of unraveling could be done by people working on their own, without professional help. That is how I came to write this book.

"Unraveling" means finding the person you were before marriage and discovering the person you became as a result of the relationship. It also means deciding which behavior patterns of your past you want to keep and develop, and which are unhealthy, painful or limiting and must be either eliminated or changed.

This is not to say that armed with this book you can be your own counselor or psychiatrist and cope with serious emotional problems. But I believe the book can provide a guide to understanding the patterns that led to your problems in love and marriage, as well as providing a plan to avoid those problems.

Unraveling will help those of you who are coming out of a broken marriage, as well as those who are emerging from an affair and wondering why, however rosy the beginning, the end is always the same. If you are still married but are considering divorce, unraveling may provide some needed directions before you take the step. For you who are divorced but who have not yet learned to enjoy your new freedom, I hope that what you read will help you realize that being single is a viable state, and for some, the best possible one. Unraveling should also help those of you who have not yet married for the first time but would like to look forward to a marriage that will last.

Although I discuss the emotional debris a divorce leaves in its wake, I do not discuss the problems of alimony, division of property, or the really difficult ones involving children. The emphasis here is on *you,* and how to get yourself in focus.

There is an important point to consider before you undertake unraveling. A good divorce demands not only the legal severance of two people via a legal contract, it also demands the severance of emotional dependency. It no longer matters what your former spouse thinks about what you are doing or planning to do, or whether he or she likes you or not. You must stop acting as if your ex-partner is still in the picture, silently exerting an influence on your behavior, editing your responses. In unraveling yourself, you are on your own and you should take advantage of your freedom to think independently. This may be easy for you or difficult, depending upon what stage of your post-divorce adjustment you are in. During all my years of clinical practice I have never met a person who was not emotionally scarred by the process of separation and divorce. Whether you welcomed or dreaded your divorce, whether you initiated the proceedings or had them forced upon you, the final separation arouses painful and conflicting emotions. No matter how difficult the relationship may have been, its end is perceived as a loss. It no longer exists—someone significant has left your life.

Psychology qualifies as a science because human beings exhibit common behavior under certain circumstances which falls into predictable patterns. In the case of divorce, the patterns are universal enough to permit generalization, and it is important for you to recognize that many of the feelings you have following a divorce are not yours alone. You are covering well-trodden ground as you wander through this maze of emotions. Accept what you are feeling, and regard it as natural pattern of readjustment.

In my observation these post-divorce symptoms follow stages. You may experience these stages in different order, but most people go through all of them.

Trauma. It occurs the moment one partner introduces the word "separation" or "divorce" for the first time. The prospect of being alone is frightening. You feel as if you are falling apart, wonder if you can survive alone (or if the one waiting in the wings is a mistake after all), that life is unfair, that you have failed, that you'll never trust anyone again and that you should have made it work somehow for the sake of the children, the family, your friends, and even the neighbors, who you now imagine saw you as an "ideal" couple.

You may burst into tears over nothing, get hysterical, break things or start a fight. If you're the one being left, you may beg for explanations, another chance to work things out, and you may even grovel. If you are the instigator, you may find you are so full of guilt that you can't eat or sleep, much less prepare for a bright new future. In either case you'll talk compulsively, rehashing, justifying and explaining "my position" to anyone who will listen.

You'll suffer from headaches, heartburn, rapid heartbeat, even toothache, and you'll find yourself reaching for aspirin, tranquilizers, antacid or martinis . . . anything to ease the pain.

That you are an adult and believe you "should" be in control and obviously are not is often harder to take than the separation itself. But again, you have company.

Interviews with insurance companies in three Eastern states reveal that people who apply for coverage during the first year following divorce are considered high risks and are unlikely to be insured. The incidence of car and home accidents rises significantly during this period, and physical examinations before the divorce are often invalidated afterward.

After the initial shock, blame-taking and blame-giving alternate with no apparent logic. One day it's all the other person's fault. The next it's yours.

Anger. Then, when you have just about gone under, the instinct for survival takes over and you get angry. A good healthy ego-restoring anger is a strong tool for survival. You will show him/her. You have fantasies of getting even, of telling your soon-to-be-ex all the things you always held back. You even consider physical violence. Such feelings help you get through the day—and the night, which is usually worse.

Numbing. This is another stage and another tool for survival. You pull out of the emotional arena and allow yourself to regroup psychologically and physically. Numbing does not heal; it's like putting a Band-Aid over a fracture. It's a way of playing it safe, not gambling on anything that provokes deep feeling.

Making up for lost time. But sooner or later this self-imposed withdrawal becomes too difficult to maintain. You begin to feel that somehow, during or because of marriage, you missed out on some wonderful experiences. You decide to make up for lost time by frantic activity. Bed- or bar-hopping are common, if temporary, solutions. You shuffle in and out of numbness and sometimes into the world of fantasy, still afraid to make forward strides.

Roller coaster. This is a difficult stage to get through—your emotions vacillate between calm and turmoil. The periods of calm are longer now, but the unprovoked emotional outbursts can be devastating. For example, you may be enjoying a delightful dinner party, excuse yourself, walk into the bathroom, look in the mirror and start crying bitterly. Nothing tangible has set you off. You are merely overwhelmed by hopelessness.

Reaching out. At this stage it is still difficult to do much with other people on your own initiative. But you can be in situations structured by someone else which are not too demanding in terms of one-to-one interaction. You might enroll in a course, take up karate, join a consciousness-raising group or a health club, develop a hobby or do volunteer work. It's most important that you push yourself to make new friends and to risk new experiences. You're not ready for real closeness, but you're gratified by a show of interest.

Revolving relationships. The positive feedback you receive about yourself while working through the previous stages will enable you to enter relationships a little more deeply and for longer periods of time. You will be wise to seek involvement with various people to test your capacity to relate and to determine what kind of relationship will serve you best. Each new relationship will contribute to your knowledge about yourself.

At first this highly conscious method of relating to a variety of people may seem artificial, as though you were role-playing. But it's a significant stage for future development. These revolving relationships prepare us for more intimate ones when we are ready for them.

It is impossible to predict how long each stage will last or how long it will take you to feel whole again. Some people move quickly from one stage to another and then, under stress or when confronted by a negative experience, regress.

If you have experienced some or all of the "stages," your emotions have leveled off, and you are ready for the next step: finding yourself again through unraveling—before you marry again.

Acknowledgments

I have worked most closely with my agent-writer, Connie Clausen. She is a multitalented person who is wise as well as creative. My thanks to Arthur Lewis and Bernard A. Bergman, who, independently, introduced me to her.

Norma Lee Clark, a gifted friend with boundless energy, made significant contributions. To her, I am deeply grateful.

My thanks also to Charlotte Mayerson, my editor, who in her inimitable style guided me and others involved with all phases of the production of this work.

I wish to express my gratitude to Sallie Murphy for her efforts, support and encouragement during my writing of this book.

Creative output requires technical proficiency and other outside supports. My thanks to Cheryl Wainer, who typed an early manuscript; to Elaine Ellick, my secretary, for her loyalty, dependability and efficiency; to Carolyn Lumsden, assistant to the editor, who expedited many necessary details; and to Dorothy Skarzynsk, for her meticulous proofreading and insightful comments.

Contents

Part One

Find Your Pattern

One

The Pattern Principle

True love has come at last,
And all before a sham;
True the name and the face have changed,
But look again with morning eye—
At the soul behind the face
The man behind the name.
The pattern again repeats itself—
Alas, he is the same.
                                        —ANONYMOUS

Have you ever wondered why . . .

· some people are drawn only to those who
reject them or treat them badly?
· some men exchange one domineering wife
for another?
· some women persist in marrying alcoholics
or other addictive personalities?
· some men and women can only relate to a
partner who is socially or intellectually
beneath them?
· some people go from one disastrous love
affair or marriage to another, never seeming
to learn from their past mistakes?

The answer is—they are all repeating patterns. Some are
merely re-enacting old and unresolved conflicts by choosing
as a partner a person who resembles the parent with whom
they are still struggling internally. For example, a woman
may spend her childhood in a series of battles with her

father, then choose a husband as much like her father as possible and re-create the earlier situation. Her marriage becomes another battlefield as she fights to win the unfinished war with her father.

Others are striving to find in their lovers or mates what they could never get from their parents. The neglected little boy may grow up to demand nonstop mothering from his wife. *She* will have to make up to him for all the love he didn't receive from his mother.

And still others are merely imitating the patterns set by their parents. A domineering woman may be imitating her much-admired mother, who ran her family with great firmness and accepted no back talk. It worked for her mother, therefore it is the "right" way to do things.

These patterns are seldom consciously chosen, but they are powerful nevertheless. It is often easier to see these behavior patterns in others than it is to see them in ourselves. Yet we are all, to a greater or lesser degree, prisoners of our past. Eric Berne, in *Transactional Analysis in Therapy*, proposes that we all have "tape recordings" stored in our brains consisting of everything our parents told us we should do. Nagy and Spark, family therapists, have written about each person's loyalty to the "family of origin" and how it conflicts with loyalty to the present family.

One of the clearest examples of the re-enactment pattern is Wendy, a woman who came to me when she was about twenty-seven, after several unsatisfactory love affairs and a divorce. "I only fall in love with men who don't love me," she complained, "and I get hurt every time. It started in school. I always had a crush on some boy who didn't know I was alive. I'd dream up elaborate schemes to get his attention. I did one boy's homework for a year. He didn't even say thank you, much less ask me for a date."

As an adult, Wendy had love affairs that followed the same pattern: unconsciously, she sought out men who rejected her, very much the way her mother had rejected her throughout her childhood. Why would she want to repeat a situation that caused her unhappiness in the past? She didn't simply want to repeat it, she wanted to rectify it. Each time she fell in love she believed it would be different, each time she tried to bring about a happy ending, but were she to choose a man who loved her, she could not re-enact the drama that still engaged her.

The men she selected were not aware of her quest and may not have set out to hurt her, but they, like her mother, were caught up in their own problems. Wendy's incessant demands for affection only irritated them and drove them further away. So she tried harder, suffering very real anguish at every rejection, and experiencing a sick kind of joy at every crumb of "love" she managed to obtain.

Of course, Wendy's conception of what constitutes love is erroneous. To her, any love worth having must be worked hard for as she worked to gain her mother's love. Like many children in similar circumstances, Wendy believed that her mother's rejection of her must be her fault: she was simply not pretty or good or lovable enough. Since her father had deserted them shortly after her birth, she was entirely helpless and dependent upon her mother, so it was not surprising that she took this responsibility; if she protested or blamed her mother, her mother might grow angry and leave her. Also, blaming herself gave her a measure of control over her situation. If it was *her* fault, she reasoned, it was not altogether hopeless; by being "good," she could still hope to win her mother's love and be safe.

As she grew older she continued to cling to the belief that she was somehow lacking and to her need for love at any price. A deep sense of deprivation colored her life, and determined to rewrite her history, she began her quest for a partner who duplicated her mother as much as possible.

Ironically, even if she were to win and succeed in getting the love she craves from a husband or lover, she wouldn't want it, or would ultimately find it suffocating, because it would be the love of a parent for a child, and Wendy is no longer a child and no longer really in need of mother love. When she recognizes this, she will be able to break the pattern.

The man who exchanges one domineering woman for another may be postponing his adulthood by marrying a woman exactly like his mother. His wife may nag, but nagging may be the only kind of "love" he has ever known, so he feels comfortable with it. Were she to stop nagging, he would see it as a sign that she no longer cared about him.

There may be other factors at work in this kind of marriage, as there were in Robert's. His mother had been an extremely controlling woman, who constantly made him feel inadequate. Never able to express how angry this made him, he was virtually filled with rage and deeply hostile toward women. Since he had had little chance to develop initiative or strength, he remained a totally dependent personality. Dependency and anger are inevitably intertwined.

In marrying a woman who dominated him, he fulfilled two needs: his need to be taken care of and his need to express his rage. He did this by rejecting his wife physically: "How can I make love to a woman who nags all the time?"

The woman who marries an alcoholic is often the daughter of an alcoholic. Perhaps she has grown accustomed to being strong and taking care of someone "weaker"—a position it is not easy to abandon. Or the reasons may be more subtle. Alcoholics, addicts of any kind, are unable to stand a close relationship, and often, so are the people they marry.

Helen spent twelve lonely years married to a heavy drinker before she summoned the courage to get out. Once divorced, she vowed to find a man who was the exact opposite of her husband, one who never went near a bar or drank, even socially. Her second husband was a serious, hard-working teetotaler, but before the year was over, Helen realized she had married another kind of addict. Work was his Scotch; the office, where he spent fourteen hours a day, his bar. He was a classic "workaholic."

Helen was drawn to the addictive personality, to men who would not or could not get too close. She wanted love, but she was afraid of it.

The man who can only relate to women socially or intellectually beneath him may be working out a conflict with his father. He knows he will infuriate his father by his choice, but he may be unable to express his anger toward him any other way. Conversely, he may be afraid of angering his father by overtaking him, so he settles for less.

A woman may be afraid of topping her mother. Dorothy, a successful physicist, was married to a man who could only be called, and often was, a complete boor. He so obviously felt inferior to her and threatened by her position that he never missed an opportunity to humiliate her in public. Her friends were overjoyed when he finally went too far and she divorced him.

Her opinion of herself has not altered, however. Although her new lover is far younger than her first husband, he too makes sure she stays in what he believes is her place—at his feet. In both instances, Dorothy's role is a replay of the one she played with her mother, a beautiful woman who wanted no competition. As much as Dorothy suffers, she feels safe this way. Although she has fame, she is not a success as a woman because of her failures with men. She therefore has not surpassed her mother, nor risked reliving her early terror of being abandoned. By limiting what she allows herself to have in her personal life, she has given herself permission to be a success in her work. If she allowed herself to have love *and* success, she would feel guilty and frightened.

This kind of balancing act is very common with women in our society who often cannot quite believe they *can* have the whole pie. They feel they must pay for every triumph in business with a corresponding humiliation in their personal life. Some will go to great lengths to keep this mythical balance sheet in order. It is as if they were saying, "I can have this, but not that. I can make a good salary, be happy in my work, but I must pay for it somehow, or Mother will be angry and leave me." These women can often juggle corporations but find themselves unable to balance their checkbooks or to keep their income-tax records in order. They maintain their helplessness in one area of their lives so they can continue to believe they must have someone to "take care of them." They will continue this pattern of denial until they can accept who they are and feel entitled to the whole package.

This pattern usually begins, as it did with Dorothy, with a mother or father who is overtly or covertly jealous of or threatened by their child's accomplishments or beauty, believing that it takes something away from them. To carry this further, little girls often fear being beautiful or gifted because they may steal their father away from their mother. They then spend their lives trying to keep a low profile, to hide their talents or gifts. They are careful not to shine in all areas lest they arouse their mother's jealousy. "Don't worry, Mamma, I won't do better than you did, or take Daddy away. I'm not really a threat. Don't leave me." If the father is the key figure, the dialogue may become, "I'm not so smart, Daddy. I still need you."

Repeating patterns can have a positive side. Marrying someone who embodies the characteristics of a beloved or admired parent makes a certain amount of sense—as long as we relate to our spouse as an adult and not as we related to the original model when we were children. Too often, however, we choose mates who have the qualities we actually despised or feared in our parents. The more difficult they were to deal with in our childhood, the more tempting it is to go into the arena again—and the marriage becomes a contest.

Mary McCarthy described this kind of marriage brilliantly in her novel *The Company She Keeps*, wherein an analyst confronts the heroine with the fact that in choosing her present husband, a man who is extremely critical of her, she has shown a tremendous amount of courage because she has dared to take on the aspect of her father's character that she feared the most. The story is psychologically accurate, and I have seen variations of it enacted over and over again with the participants being completely unaware that they were fighting old wars. It is a little like getting back on a horse that has just thrown you.

It is not only women who repeat such patterns. A young man may marry an extremely aggressive woman, although this same kind of aggressiveness in his mother embarrassed him and made him profoundly uncomfortable as a boy. Now, in marrying "his mother," he imagines that he is strong enough to change her, to mold her into the mother he wanted her to be. In brief, he will direct this new drama to a satisfying last act in which he emerges strong and wise, and his wife (mother) is chastened and respectful of him. In the same manner, the young man may also have a secret envy of his mother's "toughness," a quality which he lacks or believes to be unattractive. His wife can then be tough and aggressive *for* him and he need never acknowledge that "soft" side of himself.

Some patterns are imitated or borrowed from our parents because the patterns worked for them. Fred, twenty-five years old, clearly wanted a girl "just like the girl who married dear old Dad." Like his father, Fred required a lot of freedom, but he wanted the stability of a home and a wife to return to when he was tired or hungry or needed bolstering, just as his father had come home to his mother when he was through playing. He wanted, in effect, a "mother" more than a wife. And he found one in Peggy, who, like his mother, was overweight but not over-demanding.

In a culture devoted to weight-watching, their marriage was a constant topic of discussion among their friends. When Peggy added another thirty-five pounds to an already overburdened frame, everyone felt sorry for Fred. He was successful, good-looking, outgoing—and slim. Why did he put up with a woman who kept bursting out of her clothes and seemed content to stay that way? Why didn't Fred do something about it? Why didn't she?

His well-meaning friends finally intervened and talked Peggy into going on a diet. She lost weight, bought a new wardrobe and talked about getting a job. She also stopped being an all-purpose cook, housecleaner and "mother" to Fred, and began demanding he spend time with her or take her with him on his many nights out.

Fred became morose and depressed and everyone was astonished. "I liked her the way she was," he said. Of course he did. Peggy, overweight and unattractive, gave him a built-in excuse to leave her at home and pursue his own fancies—go to the races, play all-night poker, and on occasion take out other women.

Peggy opted to stay thin, got a job and the marriage broke up. Two years later Fred was again happily married to a double of the pre-diet Peggy, in temperament as well as size, and Fred is again a man about town. His new wife comforts herself, as Peggy once did, by overeating, which may be the only thing she can do if she wants to hang on to Fred and the marriage. This time his friends stay out of it. Fred has found a pattern that works, at least as long as he can get his wife to cooperate.

There are people who consciously determine *not* to repeat their parents' patterns, which they perceived as negative, and yet find they have unconsciously repeated them, after all. Joan's story is typical, even though not many women would have been as tenacious in acting it out as Joan was.

Although her father was "weak" and had been unable to make a living, Joan adored him and disliked her mother, primarily because she felt her mother had destroyed her father's confidence by flaunting her superior strength and intelligence. Joan made up her mind she would not be like her mother, so she was determined to marry a strong man, whom she would not be able to "destroy." When she married she vowed she would be submissive and make her husband feel important. Yet three times her marriages ended in disaster. "My husbands seemed to be so different, but they were all alike," she said. "Why couldn't I see it?"

Perhaps because appearances *are* deceiving. Jamie, her first husband, six foot two and handsome, fit the romantic artist stereotype. Clive, number two, a tidy, driven businessman, was outwardly as different from Jamie as humanly possible. Sam, her husband number three, was big, expansive and *macho*. But beneath these different exteriors they had two basic things in common: each had had a strong, domineering mother and each wanted a strong, domineering wife to take care of him. All of them hid this need with varying degrees of effectiveness, and in each instance Joan found that the strong man she longed for was in reality a dependent personality.

On another level, however, Joan knew precisely what she was doing in choosing these men. She feared, subconsciously, that if she had indeed found a strong man, she might lose her self in the marriage. By choosing weak men, she guaranteed her ultimate freedom from them because the marriages would not work and she'd have to rescue herself. In other words, Joan had to give herself a reason to be the strong woman she was. Without this excuse, she believed she would be like her mother.

One could ask, How and why did Joan's husbands choose her? Because Joan, too, was deceiving. Between her marriages she would be an extremely successful, bright businesswoman. The moment she said "I do," however, she transformed herself into what she believed a good wife should be, to her husbands' constant bewilderment. They had perceived Joan's inner strength quite accurately and were all dumfounded when she persisted in denying it.

Each of these cases illustrates what I have come to call the Pattern Principle.

We cannot change our past, nor would we really want to re-create it if we could, because our needs as adults are different. But we can take charge of our present by understanding the patterns that led to our difficulties.

The following questions will help you determine the *kind* of pattern you followed in your last relationship.

1. In retrospect, who was your last partner most like in temperament—your mother or your father?
2. Were you consciously aware of this before marriage?
3. Did you admire the parent your partner most resembled?
4. When your partner became angry, how did you respond?
5. Did you respond this way with one of your parents? Which one?
6. When your partner expressed or withheld love, how did you react?
7. Did you react this way with one of your parents? Which one?
8. In your relationship:
    Did you call your wife "Mother"?
    Did you call your husband "Father"?

9. In your childhood, who was the boss—your mother or your father?
10. How did you feel about this?
11. Who was the boss in your last relationship?
12. Did this cause conflict?
13. Did you consciously model yourself on an admired parent? Which one?
14. Did you consciously try to be as different as possible from one of your parents? Which one?
15. Have you ever felt or sounded (tone of voice, exact words) like one of your parents?

Two

Find Your
Behavior Pattern

O NE of the most important steps in getting to know yourself is to think about how you behaved during times of conflict in your last relationship.

DID YOU USUALLY GIVE IN?
DID YOU USUALLY WITHDRAW?
DID YOU USUALLY ATTACK?

Whichever pattern you followed, it was undoubtedly the one that worked best for you as a child.

Each of us develops a singular behavior pattern in order to help us cope with life, to ensure survival and, we hope, to grow. When our environment is healthy, we respond in kind, sometimes we seek love and approval, sometimes we choose to withdraw, to run from involvement. And sometimes we are aggressive and even hostile. All three responses are appropriate at different times and even essential to our growth and to maintaining sound relationships with others. In her classic book, *Neurosis and Human*

Growth, Karen Horney describes these three adaptive "solutions" as moving *toward*, moving *away from* or *moving against* people.

The problem is that we do not live in an entirely healthy society. Many of us grow up in a home environment lacking love and warmth, or one that is smothering, or one that is actually hostile and possibly dangerous. Depending on our temperament, our circumstances, our gifts and our imagination, we find a style of behavior that helps us to cope—to stay safe—and to find some measure of love. As time passes, many of us tend to depend almost exclusively on one behavior pattern, or "solution," and cling to it for dear life, whether or not it is appropriate or even effective. It is as if three small, unarmed children were approached by a ferocious bear which later, for reasons of its own, ambled away. One child may have offered the bear honey and thereafter believed that giving will keep him safe. The second child may have covered his face and pretended the bear wasn't there; he then deduced that detachment is the best defense. The third child may have shouted and waved a stick; after his apparent success with the bear, he goes through life using a club whenever threatened.

A key step in your unraveling after a divorce will be to determine which of these "solutions" is typical of your own behavior pattern. I have found the quiz that follows most helpful in my clinical practice, not only for determining this pattern but for stimulating my clients to think about how the pattern developed, about the effect it may have had on their previous relationships and whether it is still influencing their behavior.

This is a forced-choice quiz. You *must* pick one answer, though it may not be what you would always do in all situations. Decide, instead, what your most common response would be. Bear in mind that there are no right or wrong answers, no "ideal" responses.

THE QUIZ

1. During my elementary-school days, if my mother said, "I know you want to go out with your friends, but it's too late now and you'll have to stay home," I probably:
   - (a) Protested a little, but finally gave in
   - (b) Told myself I didn't want to go anyway
   - (c) Said, "I don't care, I'm going," maybe followed by a temper tantrum

2. During my last marriage, when my spouse and I argued, I usually:
   - (a) Apologized and asked to be forgiven
   - (b) Refused to argue and walked away
   - (c) Became verbally (sometimes physically) abusive

3. If a disagreement threatens a friendship, I:
   - (a) Give in, in order to avoid further unpleasantness
   - (b) Pretend nothing has happened
   - (c) Never give in if I know I'm right

4. As a child in school activities I:
   - (a) Joined the strongest person or group
   - (b) Stayed on the sidelines
   - (c) Led the group and initiated the action

5. I see myself as a person who:
   - (a) Likes to be liked by others and in their company
   - (b) Likes to be by myself
   - (c) Likes to influence others

6. My feelings about romantic love are:
   - (a) I love to be in love . . . and to show it.
   - (b) It's okay . . . as long as it doesn't get too heavy.

    (c) I can give love . . . if it's not *demanded* of me.

7. When I get upset I:
   (a) Look for someone sympathetic to talk to
   (b) Try to put it out of my mind
   (c) Get angry, usually end up by upsetting others

8. When my boss criticizes my work I:
   (a) Work overtime to correct the mistakes
   (b) Resent it deeply, though I never show it
   (c) Defend my work and counterattack

9. When I am sexually frustrated I:
   (a) Pretend that I was satisfied and feel responsible for the failure
   (b) Turn my attention to other areas: work, sports, etc.
   (c) Feel my partner let me down and let him/her know it by my words or by my silence

10. When someone points out a fault in me I:
    (a) Feel hurt and defensive
    (b) Numb it out
    (c) Become annoyed or angry

11. I work best:
    (a) As part of a team
    (b) Alone
    (c) When I'm in charge

12. When I complete an important job at work or at home I:
    (a) Wait for approval and compliments
    (b) Go on to the next job
    (c) Make certain everyone knows I did it

13. At parties I usually:
    (a) Spend most of my time helping to serve and clean up

(b) Drift to a corner and sit quietly

(c) Make sure I'm where the action is

14. People who know me well consider me:
    (a) Soft and good-natured
    (b) Difficult to get to know
    (c) Strong and self-confident

15. If a storekeeper shortchanges me five cents, I would:
    (a) Be too embarrassed to ask for it
    (b) Consider it not worth the hassle
    (c) Point out the error and demand it back

16. When I get angry I:
    (a) Feel ashamed
    (b) Reason myself out of it
    (c) Yell and get it off my chest

17. I like to be with people who:
    (a) Need me
    (b) Are self-sufficient
    (c) Depend on me

18. When I get a cold I:
    (a) Go to bed and hope for pampering
    (b) Try to ignore it and hope everyone else will also
    (c) Become impatient and angry

19. It's easiest for me to express anger:
    (a) On someone else's behalf
    (b) By letter or telephone
    (c) Face to face

20. My motto would probably be:
    (a) All the world loves a lover
    (b) Don't make waves
    (c) To the victor belong the spoils

How to Score: Count the number of your (a), (b) and (c) responses. If the majority of your responses was (a), you tend to respond as a DOVE; if the majority was (b), you have an OSTRICH personality; and if the majority was (c), your response is that of a HAWK.

If you have scored with, say, 15 (a) answers and 5 (b) and no (c), it is easy to see that you are primarily a Dove with a few Ostrich traits and *no* Hawk tendencies. However, if you have scored 8 (a) answers, 9 (b) answers and 3 (c) answers, you are almost equally a Dove and an Ostrich, with a bit of a Hawk. This is because although you may lean primarily in one direction, you can be a Hawk in some circumstances and a Dove in others, and an Ostrich in still others.

---◇---

Doves

Giving, loving, gentle, sensitive, Doves *need love.* Their happiness and security depend upon the love of just about everybody—and if it costs them themselves, for Doves the price it right.

Self-sacrificing, self-effacing and ever so humble, they do for others what they secretly wish others would do for them. That's because it's hard for them to ask for anything outright. They dream of finding a special someone who will understand their needs without their ever having to express them. Of course there are no mind readers, so Doves often wind up disappointed. The search for this special someone, be it wife, husband, friend or lover, consumes the energies Doves might better use to find and fulfill themselves. Meanwhile they often play subordinate when they could be boss, and swallow their own dreams to boost others to the top. It's not that they're really inferior, it's that they feel safer behind the throne than on it, and they'd rather be loved than be President.

Doves are absolute rocks of reliability. They are always there to do the dirty work no one else wants to do, and always there to shoulder the responsibility and the blame. "*Mea culpa*" could be their battle cry as they rush forward to confess it was all their fault—and apologize when someone steps on their toes.

Gentle and peace-loving, Doves soothe sore tempers and rarely lose their own. They vent their anger at themselves instead, by catching colds, losing their wallets and carving their fingers instead of the pot roast. Doves are dependable and loyal, and if they sound too good to be true, it's because they often are—too good to be true to themselves.

Ostriches

Cool, judicious, detached and distant, Ostriches need space. If anyone comes too close, they run, and they are among the fastest runners on earth. They also do what the ostrich is more popularly thought to do: to avoid confrontation—or worse, disappointment—they bury their heads, and their hearts and their gifts.

Because their detachment takes so many forms, they are the hardest to pin down. Sometimes they run from the world, sometimes they merely run, and sometimes they simply sit (preferably in front of a moving screen). They turn up in various roles: the ivory-tower dreamer, the office flirt, the rugged individualist or the rebellious drifter. Since escape is their goal, they can also be charming alcoholics or gadabouts lost in a numbing social whirl.

Those who marry them know best that life with an Ostrich can be a little cold. Ostriches may show up with flowers as long as someone is there to greet them, all dressed up and smiling. But they're nowhere to be found the day a good friend is fired or his doctor tells him the X-rays suggest surgery. They're not heartless, they really believe the other person "wouldn't want me to see him like that."

Ostriches prefer to suffer in silence—and alone. Resignation is the bitter pill they swallow; if they don't expect too much, they can't be disappointed, and if they don't try too hard, no one can say they've failed. No strings, no ties, no obligations. Contracts, leases, timetables are the enemy, and even Christmas makes them anxious.

Dreamers, philosophers, visionaries or escapists, their detachment gives them an integrity that the Dove, driven to please, and the Hawk, driven to succeed, may lack. But detachment also cuts them off from the best in others and in themselves.

----------◇----------

Hawks

Driven, ambitious, decisive and brave, Hawks *need power*. In pursuing their goals, they may make a lot of enemies, but they also get a lot accomplished along the way. Their hostility, aggressiveness and occasional paranoia make them tough to live with, but they keep everyone on their toes, and often we admire them.

They admire themselves, too. Hawks often really are superior. They seek bind obedience, unswerving loyalty and plenty of admiration, but then, they work harder and longer than anyone else, so they usually deserve it. Besides, Hawks have an undeniable magnetism; they cover their competitiveness with impeccable manners and considerable charm.

Hawks are perfectionists, and since they strive to perfect themselves, they find it hard to understand that everybody doesn't want to follow their example. Although they are critical of others—and themselves—they don't respond well to criticism. Any suggestion that they may just possibly be wrong not only triggers their rage, it can throw them into a deep depression. For under that Super-Hawk façade, they know they're not as tough as they appear to be. This double bind makes Hawks a mystery. They are up one minute, down the next, and when they seem the most benign, they may only be warming up for a showdown. But that's what makes them fascinating.

Although Hawks believe might is right, they're surprisingly fair-minded. They don't judge others more harshly than they judge themselves, and seldom ask anyone to do more than they would do.

To Hawks the world's a battle ground and they're surrounded by enemies. But they needn't worry—they come armed with insight, are born strategists and have the force of dynamos. The only battles they can't win are with themselves.

These portraits of Doves, Ostriches and Hawks deliberately stress the *problem-making* aspects of your personality. If you are a Dove, you may say, "Okay, so I give too much, but I am loving." An Ostrich could defend himself or herself as being judicious. And a Hawk may protest, "Maybe I'm too aggressive, but it's people like me who make the world go round." And each would be right. Each category does have positive aspects. Moving toward, away from or against other people are not necessarily ineffective interpersonal strategies. It depends on how one uses them.

"Moving toward" can characterize a lover who is not frightened by responsibility, a family man or woman who assumes an "all for one and one for all" philosophy; a member of a group who spends countless hours working for a political objective with others; or a person capable of a deep, sincere friendship based upon dependability and loyalty.

We can all recognize that there are times when it makes more sense to withdraw from a situation or an emotional confrontation than to remain. It can be an indication of maturity and good judgment. Often personal discipline is required to move away from a potential fight in a public place. Leaving the scene temporarily until you and the other person cool off can be effective in maintaining a relationship.

Moving against others can be an expression of nonconformity, of individualism, of healthy independence of thought and action. Positive examples of moving against others are exhibited by being assertive regarding personal rights, having the ability to say no and mean it, disciplining children when they need it or initiating a political countermovement. A healthy personality is one that responds appropriately at different times to different circumstances.

This is not to say that being a Hawk at business and a Dove in love is necessarily healthy. Both may be Hawk or Dove in the extreme. For example, a man may be extremely aggressive and Hawk-like in his business dealings and be very much an Ostrich in close personal relationships, being unable to respond to any emotional demands a wife or lover may make upon him. Or he may become completely Dove-like on the home front, not considering women to be serious competition. He then feels free to drop his Hawk personality and be "mothered" and catered to.

A woman can follow similar patterns, being smart and aggressive in business but reverting to Dove-like "feminine" attitudes in her close relationships with men. Ostriches also take on different attributes. Their reserved, detached exterior may conceal a passionate, sexually aggressive Hawk Lover.

It is when the personality is tilted too far in one direction that problems arise in relating to others. The Hawks we are describing believe that they *have* to be perfect or right or in control at all times. They must win by any means, and if they don't, they are crushed and humiliated beyond what would be a normal reaction. We all like to win, but we are not totally devastated if we lose. We may like to run things, but we don't perceive all those in authority as potential enemies.

We all wish to withdraw at times; to be able to detach ourselves from a situation may be the only way to gain perspective. But we do not find *any* closeness a source of terror. We welcome genuine intimacy and sharing at certain moments that to an Ostrich would be claustrophobic.

We all like to give, to sacrifice occasionally for the sake of another person without any thought of reward. But our giving is not conditional, and not desperate, as is the Dove's. And somehow we know the difference.

Three

Acting Out

WHATEVER you found your primary behavior pattern to be, it is important for you to recognize how you got that way; why you narrowed your behavior so drastically; what it cost in terms of your happiness; and how it stands in the way of your making it with another person.

It is also helpful for you to recognize these behavior responses in other people. Now that you have taken the quiz in the preceding chapter and found your basic behavior pattern, try answering the questions as you think your former spouse would have answered them. It may give you some insights on where you both were in your relationship.

If you find you are a Dove and your "ex" fits the Hawk portrait, don't be surprised; you were attracted in the first place to a strong, tough person whom you hoped would make up for what you weren't. The snarl probably came about when you began to show the other side of your Dove nature (inside every Dove lies a sleeping Hawk), or you got tired of all that aggression, or the Hawk in your partner simply got bored with too much submission from you and set off to make a new conquest.

Although all Doves tend to give in order to get, Hawks to strike before they are struck, and Ostriches to keep their distance, each of them acts out these basic orientations in a different way. In this chapter we will give you a fuller picture of all three types, and how they got that way.

———◇———

Doves

Dove Lovers

This first category of Doves represents modern-day Emma Bovarys and Romeos and Juliets. Dove Lovers live for love and sometimes die for it.

"I'm only half alive when I'm not in love," they are fond of saying, and it's true that for them the times when they are not in love are seen as dry stretches, barren and devoid of meaning.

Possessed and preoccupied by the idea of love, Dove Lovers, like addicts, need the "fix" of love, real or imagined. They can apparently never get enough or give enough. In fact, they give and get very little because the love they seek—the "unqualified love" of a parent for a child that would make them finally love themselves—is no longer attainable.

But then, Dove Lovers thrive on unrequited love. Their lovers are often married—to someone else—or they are too young or too old or too far away. This keeps Dove Love forever fresh and unsullied by the realities of everyday routine.

To merge completely with the one they love, in fact or fantasy, is all Dove Lovers' goal. Love is their antidote for anxiety, their compensation for failure, their balm for nonachievement. Love takes them "out of this world" and away from themselves, and leaves them with little time or energy to give to mundane things such as work or creative fulfillment. That's why they pursue love and endure an incredible curtailment of freedom to hang on to it. Dove Lovers reason that if they are "in love," they must be loving and therefore lovable.

Of course, they sometimes meet a fellow romantic; if the two grow to like each other along the way, they may grow to like themselves. But more often than not, they choose or are chosen by someone who is warmed by their effusive loving until the partner learns that Dove Love comes with high price tags and penalties they may not wish to pay.

WERE YOU A DOVE LOVER?

1. Were you constantly asking for reassurance that you were loved?
2. If you were criticized, did you interpret criticism as an indication that your partner was tiring of you?
3. Did you daydream about former loves and wonder how it would have been had you married them? Was this ever obvious to your partner?
4. Were you disappointed that marriage or your close relationship did not seem to be enough?
5. Did you feel you had sacrificed too much for love?
6. Did you believe you loved more than you were loved?
7. In retrospect, did you exaggerate your feeling of love?

WERE YOU MARRIED TO ONE?

1. How did you react to your partner's demands for proof of your love?
2. Were you attracted originally because your partner seemed to be so much in love with you?
3. Did you feel you did not give enough, or that your partner's demands were simply impossible to meet?

Dove Givers

Dove Givers also have a price. They may never present you with a bill, but they keep careful accounts of what they gave and what they received—or more accurately, what they *expected* and didn't receive.

Female Dove Givers have now become Total Women. They used to be called smotherers and were often accused of castrating with kindness. It is true they make life more pleasurable for their mates, but it's also true they expect a return on their investment.

The male Dove Giver is the perennial nice guy who "waits on," "waits for" and winds up with an ulcer for his efforts. He rarely gets the girl he really wants; he's so busy helping her to get what *she* wants, he doesn't notice that she's being swept off her feet by some Hawk who calls her "Baby" and demands she help *him*, or that she's enamored of an Ostrich whose indifference she finds intriguing.

Dove Givers of both sexes are perpetually asking if you want a drink, if you're warm enough, if you think you should take an umbrella. It's their way of asking you to love them for being so considerate. They buy overelaborate Christmas and birthday gifts, guaranteed to make you feel you haven't done enough (and you usually haven't, you're so furious at being forced to do anything at all). They start every other sentence with an apology, compel you to overeat because they've worked so hard preparing dinner, and literally give until it hurts—you.

They don't just give, either. They give *up*—their careers, their dreams, their personalities—in order to allow yours to flourish. And because they hate conflict, they also give *in*. They're great losers, wonderful sports and first-rate martyrs. Some also give *out* (or put out) sexually, usually on the first date. They feel they have to offer everything in order to get anything back at all. They touch too much, smile too often and try too hard, all with one aim—to be touched, smiled upon, approved of and loved in return.

Only when it's too late do you learn the cost. You are expected to provide eternal moral and financial support, love and security. You must also remain blind to the big secret all Doves strive to hide—their anger at giving in, up and out, and *getting* so little in return.

WERE YOU A DOVE GIVER?

1. Did you always give more than you received in your last relationship?
2. Did you give in order to make your spouse feel obligated? Guilty?
3. What did giving mean to you? Did you expect something in return? Were you disappointed?
4. Were you hurt when you were not appreciated? Angry?
5. Did you express your feelings on this subject?
6. How do you feel when someone seems overgiving to you? Uncomfortable? Obligated? Unworthy?
7. Were you also a giver before and outside of your marriage?

WERE YOU MARRIED TO ONE?

1. How did you react to smothering?
2. What first attracted you to a giver?
3. Did you need an excuse to withdraw or get angry?
4. Did you encourage "sacrifice," then resent it?
5. Was your mother a "giver"? Did you like her giving?

Dove Sufferers

Because the love they seek *can* never be enough, Doves may grow hostile. To reveal this would tarnish their all-loving image, so they *suffer*, physically and mentally, and so do those who love or marry them.

Psychologists call this "passive-aggressive behavior," which means Dove Sufferers may carry on a full-scale war without leaving their beds. Becoming physically ill is an almost foolproof means of punishing and controlling a partner without losing Dove status. Sometimes even their doctors don't know for sure whether Dove Sufferers are actually sick or not. Certainly they suffer real pain. A headache brought on by repressed rage is *still* a headache. And though they may find it easier to lose sleep than risk losing their temper, they still experience the torments of insomnia.

Dove Sufferers do not consciously make themselves ill, but the body is astonishingly cooperative in picking up unspoken but clear signals: "If she says one more word, I think my head will split"; "He makes me sick to my stomach"; "He won't let me breathe."

Dove Suffering is of course not limited to the body. Mental suffering can be even more painful, and give more pain to the partner. Depressions and phobias speak louder than curses, and a suicide attempt speaks loudest of all.

In effect, Sufferers are saying, "Don't ask any more of me, or I'll get sick," or, "You must take care of me because I suffer," or worse, "See what you've done to me? You're the cause of my depression."

Not surprisingly, it's difficult to persuade people who are Dove-sick to give up their suffering because they have a great deal invested in this solution. Suffering is their excuse for not doing more with their potentialities, their bill to the world for the wrongs done them, the proof that they are more sensitive than others and *special*, therefore entitled to *special* consideration. That they suffer is also punishment for their real or imagined sins and failings, and the price they pay for any success.

WERE YOU A DOVE SUFFERER?

1. How often in any month were you ill during your marriage?

2. Did you go to a physician? Did he find a legitimate reason for your complaints?
3. Did you feel that your spouse neglected you?
4. Were you able to express your anger at a real or imagined neglect?
5. Are you able now to remember a particular pain or illness and trace its development to a specific moment of feeling unloved?
6. Were you controlling your spouse through your illnesses?
7. Did you feel that complaining was the only way you could get through to him/her?
8. Did you use your illness to avoid involvement in activities that bored you? To avoid sex?

WERE YOU MARRIED TO A SUFFERER?

1. Were you aware of this propensity before marriage?
2. Do you like to take care of people?
3. Do you need to feel superior physically? Mentally?
4. Were you overly critical? Absent a great deal?
5. How did you react to complaints?

Dove Spenders

Some Doves become compulsive consumers, venting their hostility and frustration in spending sprees. This is another "passive-aggressive" way of getting even for real or imagined neglect, of filling the emptiness of a self-less life. It may also be a form of compensation for feeling unloved. There are Ostrich and Hawk Spenders also, but their motives are different, as we shall see.

Some Dove Spenders only buy for "others." They're the hardest to deal with. Since it's love they are buying, the sky is the limit, and it's hard to get angry at someone who has just wrecked the budget buying a too-expensive gift for you. Whether they are filling their closets or yours,

Dove Spenders probably cause as much havoc in marriages as the "other woman" or the "secret lover." Psychologists have even found a name for it—onomania—and since it can be as destructive as any other kind of mania, compulsive spenders may soon form groups similar to Alcoholics, Overeaters or Gamblers Anonymous—to help them break the habit.

WERE YOU A DOVE SPENDER?

1. Did you live beyond your income? What effects do you think this had on other aspects of your relationship?
2. Did you overspend before your marriage? Why?
3. Did you "do without" in order to buy gifts for your partner?
4. Did you feel more important when you made expensive purchases?
5. Did you usually give more than you received on special occasions: birthdays, Christmas, etc.?
6. Did you buy things to lift your spirits?

WERE YOU MARRIED TO A SPENDER?

1. Did you keep too tight a rein on finances?
2. Did you condone overspending because you were guilty about something you had done? Or to "buy" your freedom?
3. Were you aware of *why* your mate overspent?
4. How did you deal with the problem?

Note: You will find exercises for the various Dove types on page 108 of Chapter 7, "Take Action—Exercises," in Part Two.

DOVE CASE HISTORY

Mary had been a perfect wife in a perfect marriage. She and her husband had been high school sweethearts, and six months before he left her they had celebrated their tenth wedding anniversary.

"He gave me a silver bracelet with an inscription, 'Ten years of happiness,' and I believed it, or pretended to. I wanted our marriage to be right so desperately, I refused to see what was really going on. Our sex was terrible. I *hated* it, but I wouldn't admit it. John must have hated it too, but he was just as afraid of disturbing the status quo as I was. At least until he met that girl . . .

"I cried for days. I couldn't believe this could happen to me. I didn't want to face the neighbors or my friends because they would know I'd been living a ten-year lie."

Mary's role playing had begun long before her marriage, when she forced herself to play a happy little girl in a happy family.

Her parents maintained a front of solid togetherness in public, but in the privacy of their home they fought constantly. It was a deadly war in which Mary was the hostage, the peacemaker, and in her mind, the cause. Both parents let her know that they only stayed together for her sake, and she felt it was her responsibility to make them stop fighting and love each other. "I was a miniature Kissinger," she said, "always carrying messages of peace to the enemy."

To keep peace, she had to be achingly good. If she created any disturbance, it might set off another fight. She must be smart in school so her father wouldn't use her bad grades as a weapon against her mother. She couldn't get sick . . . "If you were a better mother, the kid wouldn't always have a cold."

Naturally, she continued this Dove pattern outside. "I was the girl who hemmed the costumes for the school play, sold the most Brownie cookies, made the highest honor points, and got to be 'best friend' of the most popular girl in class—who rewarded me by calling me Goody Two-shoes. And no wonder. I was too sweet, too understanding, too willing to forgive, too generous, too noble to be true!"

In her marriage she was afraid that if she complained about their sex, it would hurt her husband's ego, or worse, he would leave her. "I figured it was better to say nothing. But I began to dread the nights. To avoid sex I wore curlers, which John hated, or read too late, or said I was too tired." In reality, much of their sexual difficulties stemmed from John's inability to control ejaculation. But following her early pattern, Mary assumed it was her fault, that she must be frigid.

Mary glossed over other problems as well. John had a ferocious temper, which he managed to conceal from everyone but Mary. At the office he was a "good guy": he would work on holidays, lend money, do endless favors, cover for fellow employees. To his neighbors he was practically a saint: the president of the block association, the one who always cleaned his sidewalk, always paid his dues. At home, however, Mary "walked on eggs" to keep his anger under control. For her, the worst thing that could happen was divorce, so she took the full responsibility for keeping their marriage together, just as she'd done with her parents'.

In time Mary recognized that although "the worst" did happen, her life was not over and she was not destroyed. She gradually learned to accept and express her real feelings and to risk disapproval. The dissolution of her marriage was actually the beginning of Mary's life as *herself*.

Ostriches

Ostrich Lovers

Ostrich Lovers come in two varieties: one kind pursues, the other is pursued, and both seem to be successful.

Those who initiate the chase do so with cool detachment, and if they are preoccupied with love, it's quantity, not quality that seems to count. Casanova probably set the mold for this type, being sufficiently detached to keep score *and* a journal. Warren Beatty played an Ostrich lover in *Shampoo*; Liza Minnelli, the female version in *Cabaret*—both could make love without loving.

Some Ostrich pursuers are Show-Offs who use this technique to fend off intimacy. Others are Teases, more interested in the pursuit than in their quarry. Those who marry them are expected to be there when the game is over, and even to take pride in their skill. If you are foolish enough to accept this Ostrich invitation, you'll find you're up against a wall of charm that masks the hostility behind the tease.

Ostrich Lovers who are pursued tend to be more passive. Ashley Wilkes in *Gone With the Wind*, who kept Hawk Scarlett O'Hara circling endlessly and Dove Melanie devotedly standing by, is the male prototype. On the feminine side there are the roles Marlene Dietrich played in which she couldn't help it when men flocked around her "like moths around a flame"—she didn't ask them to.

WERE YOU AN OSTRICH LOVER?

1. Were you able to talk about your feelings with your partner?
2. Were you able to listen when your partner wanted to talk about his/her feelings?
3. Did you feel compelled to have more than one relationship going at one time?
4. Did you feel too vulnerable when you depended on one person for love?
5. Did you resent your partner's possessiveness?

WERE YOU MARRIED TO AN OSTRICH LOVER?

1. Do you like to feel slightly uncertain about those you love?
2. Did you enjoy always having to forgive his/her transgressions?

3. Did you think your partner's sexual adventures were a sign of his masculinity? Her desirability as a woman? Were you secretly proud?

4. Do you think you were to blame for your mate's behavior?

WERE YOU AN OSTRICH TEASE?

1. Did you feel unattractive as a child? Did you feel your parents would have loved you more if you had been more attractive?

2. Did you feel more secure about yourself when you received a positive reaction from a member of the opposite sex?

3. Did you feel more secure about yourself when your spouse was jealous?

4. What reaction did you want from your spouse when you teased? What reaction did you get? Was this gratifying?

5. Were you aware that teasing is often an expression of hostility?

WERE YOU MARRIED TO A TEASE?

1. Why were you attracted to a Tease? Did you think you could change him/her?

2. Are you sure you don't enjoy the role of martyr?

3. Was winning your mate originally a triumph for you?

WERE YOU AN OSTRICH SHOW-OFF?

1. Was your spouse embarrassed by your attention-getting behavior in public? Did he/she ever tell you this? How did this make you feel?

2. What effect did your public behavior have on your marriage?

3. Did expressions of admiration from an audience give you a sense of importance you didn't otherwise have?

4. Did you feel empty when you were alone? Did an evening alone with your spouse create anxiety? When did you first remember feeling this way? What did you do to eliminate this feeling?
5. Do you believe you are a lovable person?

WERE YOU MARRIED TO A SHOW-OFF?

1. Did you recognize this trait before marriage and find it amusing?
2. Did this behavior increase when there were problems between the two of you?
3. Are you aware that exhibitionistic actions are often hostile?
4. Did you discourage your spouse from expressing anger directly? Did you express anger directly yourself?

Ostrich Spender

The Ostrich Spender uses his pattern as an escape. Any golf or tennis widow can tell you *how* expensive an escape it is, as can her male counterpart, whose wife seems to spend all of her time and most of his money on the self-improvement circuit—from French lessons to face lifts to yoga.

Ostrich Spenders of either sex may stick to a budget in every other area but justify going all out when it comes to their favorite and "absolutely necessary" hobby, sport or collection, which is usually one they must pursue without their partner.

Another type of Ostrich Spender uses money to avoid giving of himself, substituting cash for caring, presents for presence, trips for tears. A man may send his wife on a cruise, to a spa, to Europe, but is unable to sit down quietly with her to find out what is bothering her, or even what makes her happy. In a frantic reaction against intimacy, Ostrich Spenders have been known to go bankrupt paying for luxuries the receivers could have lived without.

WERE YOU AN OSTRICH SPENDER?

1. Did you spend an inordinate amout of your income on your hobby or favorite sport?
2. How did you justify this expenditure to yourself? To your mate?
3. Do you often feel that you deserve to indulge yourself because you work so hard, or are under so much pressure?
4. Did you buy overelaborate gifts because you felt you failed in other areas?

WERE YOU MARRIED TO AN OSTRICH SPENDER?

1. Did your partner's overspending begin before or after marriage?
2. Do you feel that you contributed to your partner's overspending?
3. Did you encourage your partner's overspending by demanding too much attention? Or by not giving him/her enough attention?
4. Did you often praise your partner's overspending before marriage or look at it as a sign of generosity, or freedom from constraint?
5. Did your partner make you feel that you caused the overspending?

Note: Although the motives are different, the exercises for an Ostrich Spender are the same as those for the Dove Spender (see page 112).

Ostrich Tune-Out

Tune-Outs have their "on-off" switch permanently set at "off." They bury their heads in newspapers or books, are mesmerized by television, from the Super Bowl straight through to the World Series. They play golf or tennis, or go to hockey games, or go out with the "boys" or the "girls," and even those who don't leave the house still manage to tune out. They may answer your questions, but only as long as your questions don't probe too deeply.

Sometimes they pose as Intellectuals whose minds, they let you know, are on loftier levels than yours, so it's impossible to tell them the basement is flooding or even that you might be heading for a nervous breakdown. They will not be disturbed by the trivia of daily life.

They are masters at selective hearing. If something is unpleasant or requires action, they simply don't register it or they conveniently forget to take care of it. The word "problem" is not part of their vocabulary and they'll do their best to keep it out of yours.

They have convinced everyone they are delicate creatures and must be handled with care. "We mustn't bother your father [or mother] with this. He [or she] has more important things to worry about."

There are compensations, of course. Tune-Outs often have the virtue of being even-tempered. And why shouldn't they be? You are the one who is crying or coping, not they.

Tune-Outs have a reason for their behavior, although they may not know it consciously. They're afraid that if they tune in to you, you will find out their sad secret: they have long since tuned out to themselves and there is nothing much there.

WERE YOU AN OSTRICH TUNE-OUT?

1. Did you show any interest in activities and events that were important to your partner?
2. When your partner tried to reach you, did you find it impossible to respond?
3. Did you decide your spouse was so boring that the only way you could keep the relationship going was to tune out? If so, when in the marriage did this happen?

4. Do you often feel that you are "fooling" everyone, that you are not a nice person?
5. Are you afraid that if anyone really "knew" you, he/she would not like or respect you? Why?

WERE YOU MARRIED TO A TUNE-OUT?

1. Did most conversation in your marriage consist of questions or directives concerning your daily routine? Examples: "Will you take out the garbage?"; "Did you pick up the cleaning?"
2. Did you ever make any conscious effort to *talk* with your spouse?
3. Were you able to discuss your feelings with your mate? With anyone?
4. Did your partner's withdrawal serve to protect you from confronting your own problems?

Ostrich Runners

Ostrich Runners run several ways. Some, like Updike's Rabbit, run *away* from life's complexities. Others, like the original Sammy Glick, run *after* success, fame or money. Still others simply run *with* the crowd, but they all believe that if they run fast enough, nothing can hurt them.

They are the "fun" couples until they split, part of the "in" crowd until they grow old. Ostrich Runners sometimes do write a hit song or a best seller or hit a home run, and become rich and famous. Or sometimes they don't accomplish anything much. They simply *run* from job to job, town to town, marriage to marriage. Some take up causes or cults or cures, running from Left to Right. They are hippies one year, activists the next, perennial groupies, whether they follow rock stars or gurus.

The one thing they are *not* is committed. Their involvement lacks depth, and they can be turned off as quickly as they were turned on. Suddenly they realize they were "misled," so they leave the movement or the marriage and follow a new star, but they always keep a return ticket handy, just in case.

Some Runners focus on being busy. They're called busybodies, workaholics or even saints. Constantly in motion, their committees, clubs, charities and careers keep them racing, and also keep them from getting too close to anyone, including themselves.

They often seem to be such model wives and husbands and citizens that you may feel guilty when you take them away from the worthy cause that is taking them away from you.

WERE YOU AN OSTRICH RUNNER?

1. How often did you run away from your actual responsibilities to do "busy work" or join in social activities outside the home?
2. Did these activities have the highest priority in your life in terms of time and commitment?
3. How comfortable were you in intimate conversation with your spouse?
   a. Was your conversation centered on *your* activities outside the home?
   b. Did you ever discuss your feelings? Did you listen when your spouse did? How did you react?
   c. Were you comfortable spending time alone with your spouse?
   d. Did you dread spending weekends alone with him/her? Why?
4. Did your partner complain about your outside activities?
5. Did your outside activities give you a sense of importance and self-esteem? Did you feel you didn't get this from your spouse?
6. Did you hate spending time alone? Did you start phoning people if you were left alone in the house?

7. Did you take time for private moments of introspection?
8. Did you find it difficult to find something to do during unscheduled time?

WERE YOU MARRIED TO A RUNNER?

1. Did you originally encourage your mate to become involved so you could be free?
2. Were you aware that frantic overactivity was hurting your marriage?
3. Did you believe your spouse "ran" to get away from you? That it was your fault?

Ostrich Addicts

Gamblers, alcoholics, pill takers, mainliners or sniffers are probably all Ostrich Addicts—escape artists who are rarely able to handle a give-and-take relationship. In addition to the real problem of being physically addicted, they find their habit a psychological necessity to numb any deep feelings. When dealing with an addict of any kind, it is important to remember that addiction is a tool for survival and one that will not be abandoned until something is provided to take its place.

WERE YOU AN OSTRICH ADDICT?

1. Did compulsive working, gambling, smoking marijuana or drinking cause trouble in your marriage?
2. Do you always excuse yourself for these habits because of too much pressure? Worry? Work?
3. Do you feel your partner contributed to your problems? Caused them?

WERE YOU MARRIED TO AN OSTRICH ADDICT?

1. Was his or her addiction present before marriage?
2. Did you convince yourself you would "cure" the addiction?

3. Are you frequently involved with those you consider "weaker"? Why?
4. Did you ignore the problem until it was too late?

Note: You will find exercises for the various Ostrich types on page 113 of Chapter 7, "Take Action—Exercises," in Part Two.

OSTRICH CASE HISTORY

Larry was the only child of his parents' middle age, and their last chance at longed-for parenthood. His father was a silent, unassuming man, happy that he had finally been able to give his wife the only thing she wanted. His mother, from Larry's birth, fussed over him, getting up several times every night to be sure he was still breathing. His every sniffle became a drama, every scraped knee a crisis. He was quite literally smothered with love.

When be began school his mother insisted on bringing him a hot lunch, and the other children teased him and called him a mamma's boy. Because his mother was always begging him to bring his friends home after school, he began to shun the few friends he had made, knowing that she would eavesdrop on their conversations and continually interrupt with bright suggestions of what would be "fun."

In high school she was always the class mother, the chaperon at the school dances, the chauffeur who drove the kids to out-of-town football games. Larry sulked, but was unable to stop her. He soon made it a point never to tell her where he was going or where he had been, and at home spent hours lying on his bed, refusing to answer when she knocked on his door.

Although he was extremely intelligent, Larry's schoolwork began to suffer because the teachers' questions and assignments were seen by him as "demands," and any demand or pressure stirred up a terrible anger in him that he was unable to express. He turned his rage inward, telling himself he was weak and cowardly for being unable

to control his mother, or worse, that he was monstrous
to feel so much anger toward her.

On graduating, he moved to the nearest large city, got a
job as a public-school teacher and kept pretty much to
himself. The first time he allowed anyone to get at all
close to him was when he met Joanne, a fellow teacher. He
managed to keep a relationship going with her for the
sake of sex, which he found a safe bridge for human contact. However, after several months she became pregnant
and demanded that he marry her. She may have felt that
a child and her continued love would show him that it
was safe to love.

The marriage was a disaster. He resented the baby and
Joanne's constant attempts to force him to share her happiness. He had escaped one smotherer only to find another,
and he retreated, just as he had with his mother. In a year
he and his wife were divorced. Only the threat of jail and
losing his job forced him to accede to her "demands" for
child support.

In the years after his divorce, all his affairs with women
followed a similar pattern: "Things would seem good in
the beginning, the sex and everything, but as soon as I
started feeling I was doing something because they wanted
me to, I'd back off. Even if I loved the woman and wanted
to please her, I couldn't do it. I wouldn't call her, I'd
'forget' dates, and finally she would break it off. I always
tried to get the woman to make the break so I wouldn't
feel guilty."

He had, however, begun to recognize that he was caught
in a pattern of behavior toward women that made *any*
relationship impossible. The next step was to try to get in
touch with the anger he had stored up over the years. This
was difficult for him because his unexpressed anger toward
his mother had assumed gigantic proportions in his imagination. Children tend to believe that they are omnipotent
and that their angry feelings are capable of "killing" the

person to whom they are directed. It is a terrifying thought, particularly since anger at a parent could conceivably make one a murderer—and an orphan.

Because of this fear, Larry had always forced himself to "lie down" whenever he became upset. In time he no longer experienced the feeling at all. When something bothered him he merely felt "tired" or he became restless and anesthetized himself. He had to learn that as an adult he could express anger, that he was in control of his emotions and that other people were able to take care of themselves.

————◇————

Hawks

Hawk Lover

Hawk Lovers spell "love" c-o-n-t-r-o-l or c-o-n-q-u-e-r. They use sex, power or threats to win and hold the chosen one. They can be cold, or rule with passion, but rule they must. Being subject to a Hawk Lover isn't all bad, of course. They are responsible people and work hard, and will protect and care for you as long as you show you "need" them.

Hawk Lovers enjoy playing Pygmalion for their own benefit rather than yours. Like Henry Higgins, who changed his "Fair Lady" and was surprised when she wasn't grateful, or like Orson Welles's "Citizen Kane," who made his lover a star and was hurt when she objected, they don't understand why their efforts are not always appreciated. Since their pride is often greater than their love, Hawk Lovers sometimes destroy their beloved with jealousy—remember Othello and Desdemona—or weaken them, as did Delilah with her Samson.

Hawk Lovers tend to freeze or smother you, depending upon whether they were frozen or smothered as children, but either way, withdrawal is their greatest weapon. They are so sure their love is superior that they can't imagine you might be relieved if they did pull out, especially since it's nearly impossible to pull away from *them.* They too easily become indispensable.

WERE YOU A HAWK LOVER?

1. Did you believe your partner loved you more when he/she obeyed you?
2. Were you unable to feel love when your partner resisted your orders?
3. Does a pliable partner make you feel stronger, more secure?
4. When your partner gave in to you, did you sometimes feel contemptuous of him/her?

WERE YOU MARRIED TO A HAWK LOVER?

1. Do you like to be dominated? If so, why?
2. Did you ever protest?
3. Do you believe your partner was smarter than you? Stronger?
4. Who was dominant in your parents' marriage, your mother or father? Did you approve of this situation? Resent it?
5. Do you think that men should be in charge? That women should be submissive?
6. Do you think that women are basically more suited to managing a relationship?

Hawk Perfectionist

Hawk Perfectionists aren't really perfect; they need to think they are, worry that they *have* to be if they're to avoid criticism. Actually, their own criticism is probably the toughest; they know better than anyone how to whip themselves back into perfect shape—they've been practicing for years. Since the day they decided that they would never be loved or accepted for being what they *were,* they have been perfecting a new model. Naturally, they don't like to be reminded of the old one.

These Hawks are tough to live with and tough to live up to. Their closets are always ready for inspection, their homes are immaculate, their shoes and their cars shine, they never forget to fill out the check stubs, they always know precisely where the scissors are, and they don't really understand why you don't subscribe to their standards. They're willing to teach you, however, and you may be flattered to be chosen until you learn it's because they think you show so much room for improvement.

Hawk Perfectionists thrive on rules and regulations. Like Nurse Rachet in *One Flew Over the Cuckoo's Nest* and Captain Queeg in *The Caine Mutiny,* they are always trying to hold themselves together, and they tend to fall apart when the rules don't cover the situation.

They are consummate *blamers.* Since they must be perfect, anything that goes wrong *must* be someone else's fault. They don't mean to be mean, it's simply that it's you or them, and they turn on you to keep from turning on themselves.

WERE YOU A HAWK PERFECTIONIST?

1. Did you find your spouse disorganized?
2. Did you feel this as a reflection on you?
3. Did you continuously attempt to correct him/her?
4. Can you take criticism without showing anger at another person or yourself?
5. Was your divorce a result of your compulsive perfectionism?

WERE YOU MARRIED TO A PERFECTIONIST?

1. Do you enjoy being directed?
2. Did you admire your partner's high standards?
3. Were your parents critical of you? Did you resent it? Did you try to please?

WERE YOU A HAWK BLAMER?

1. How much responsibility do you assume for the incidents that eventually destroyed your marriage?
2. Did you feel that everything that went wrong in your marriage was attributable to someone else—your spouse, your mother-in-law, your parents?
3. Now that you are divorced, whom do you blame for things that go wrong?
   a. Do you turn inward and blame yourself, then punish yourself, as you once punished your partner?
4. Do you believe perfection is actually attainable?

WERE YOU MARRIED TO A BLAMER?

1. How did you respond to being attacked?
2. Did you tune out the continuous faultfinding?
3. Did you refuse to allow the blamer to "get away with it"?
4. Do you feel guilty even when blamed for something that is not your fault?
5. Were you blamed for everything that went wrong as a child? If so, by whom?

Hawk Hero/Heroine

These are the Super-Hawks, the bigger-than-life people who seem to have more stamina, more energy, more initiative than any other type. They run the show, they're the overachievers, the stars, the strong ones who seem to be impregnable. Flamboyant and charming, they're natural politicians and preachers.

They don't just try, they succeed. With them it's not the game that counts, it's the winning, and they usually win. They *have* to, for the same reasons that Hawk Perfectionists have to be perfect: to protect themselves from their greatest enemy—themselves—for beneath that champion's smile is a frightened child who might break with failure. They've been so busy running things that they haven't had time to develop any other interest to buffer them should their grandiose plans collapse. But before you run to comfort them, remember that the bricks they use to rebuild that fractured ego may be carved out of your flesh.

These Hawks can be lavish with presents, money and praise as long as you remain docile and grateful. But it's not a good idea to cross them. Your criticism is seen as hostility, and a difference of opinion as outright mutiny. Loving them doesn't always work either. Too often they think that if you love *them*, there's something wrong with you.

WERE YOU A HAWK HERO/HEROINE?

1. Were you highly competitive, even about little things, such as getting up earlier than your partner? Getting less tired? Reading faster? Being healthier?
2. Were you constantly in a contest: Who was right? Best? Strongest? Smartest?
3. If your partner seemed to win, were you depressed? Angry?
4. Did you demand that your partner recognize your "superior" abilities?
5. Did you often swing from euphoria to gloom? Was this triggered by a "failure" on your part, real or imagined?

WERE YOU MARRIED TO A HAWK HERO/HEROINE?

1. Do you tend to look for someone you can "look up to"?
2. Did you compete with your partner? If so, how did you come out? How did you feel about it?
3. How did you react when you found your hero/heroine had feet of clay? Were you derisive? Supportive? Disappointed?
4. Did you hope to live in the reflected glory of your partner?

Hawk Avengers

Getting even is almost as important to Hawk Avengers as getting to the top. They grow up believing that life has cheated them and they are determined to collect. They *never* turn the other cheek, and an eye for an eye is not quite enough. They are the men who make every woman pay for being the same sex as their mother, and the women who show men what a *man* should be.

Women Hawk Avengers never heard of the weaker sex, and Simone de Beauvoir notwithstanding, could never be rated the second one. Shakespeare's Lady Macbeth and Lillian Hellman's Regina in *The Little Foxes* are feminine prototypes. Captains Ahab of *Moby Dick* and Bligh of *Mutiny on the Bounty* were Hawk Avengers, as were Hitler and Stalin.

Less violent, but still deadly, are the Hawk *Intellectuals,* who use their superior intelligence to keep others in their place, naturally a subordinate one. They pounce on every faux pas and never hesitate to point out the errors in your thinking.

Machiavellian *manipulators* all, they enjoy setting the scene so that you lose your temper and they emerge calm, reasonable and of course victorious. When they're in a position to, they enjoy pitting their subordinates against one another in overlapping jobs and letting them fight it out. "Keeps them on their toes," they say.

Some of their actions are disguised as "taking care of you," but their aim is to control you, to "take care" according to what they think is good for you, and never mind your own desires.

They do the same thing at home, with you and the children, with your relatives, and even with theirs. Usually rigid, they can change their mind when it serves their purpose, and love to give arbitrary and contradictory orders to keep everyone around them off balance. Then they can come in and set things right again.

That their victories are hollow is already a cliché, which doesn't make it any less poignant. Hawk Avengers must be the best and brightest and the strongest, in order to finally "show them"—"them" being their parents and everyone else who didn't appreciate them or recognize their superiority, and who, sadly, failed to love them.

WERE YOU A HAWK MANIPULATOR?

1. How often did you push and probe your partner to reach some prearranged outcome?
2. Analyze your behavior with other people. Did you use this controlling mechanism in relationships other than marriage?
3. Did you feel that you really knew better than your partner what was good for him/her?

WERE YOU MARRIED TO A MANIPULATOR?

1. Did you force yourself to seem unemotional and act unconcerned in certain arguments? Did this incite your mate to greater anger?
2. Did your partner's manipulation of you absolve you of responsibilities for your actions?
3. Did you like the feeling of always being taken care of?

WERE YOU A HAWK INTELLECTUAL?

1. Did you compete intellectually with your spouse?
   a. What kind of language did you use? Did you consider it important to master technical phrases?
   b. Did you bone up on particular topics that figured in your spouse's social discussions, no matter how trivial, with the result that he/she no longer was the only expert?
2. Often it is not what you say, but how you say it that offends another person. Think about the tone and quality of your voice when you were making a point.

a. Were you sharp? Sarcastic? Emphatic in every concrete statement of fact?

b. Examine your nonverbal communication style closely. How did your body talk? Did you glare at others while speaking? Did you accentuate your ideas with a clenched fist or rapping fingers?

c. Did you consistently interrupt or contradict your spouse in social situations? How about private discussions?

3. Compare your communication with your spouse with the way you relate to other people.

a. Were you usually hostile in conversations with your spouse? If so, why?

b. Did you feel inadequate and cover these feelings with hostility? What in your background may have supported this?

WERE YOU MARRIED TO A HAWK INTELLECTUAL?

1. Did your mate's intellectual superiority give you an excuse to become lazy yourself?

2. According to your friends, how did your spouse react in situations without you?

3. Did you feel martyred having to "play second fiddle"?

4. Did you find you tuned out more and more? If so, did you do this in self-defense?

Note: You will find the exercises for the various Hawk types on page 120 in Chapter 7, "Take Action—Exercises," in Part Two.

HAWK CASE HISTORY

Hal came for help, as many Hawks do, for someone else, in this case his wife. She was drinking too much and he wanted me to tell him how to get her to stop. She was making scenes, disturbing his sleep and peace of mind, and seriously disrupting his work.

At five feet two, Hal was a Hawk by an accident of

nature as well as by temperament and the circumstances of his early environment. Had he grown up in a less stringent home, had he received more affection and support, had his schoolmates taunted him less about his height, his almost savage drive to succeed might have been less intense. But none of these mitigating factors prevailed. Hal's parents had grown up in unrelieved poverty, and in their determination to rise out of it they imposed almost inhuman standards on him as a boy. When he met their expectations they took it for granted, and he was rarely praised. The message he got was: Be smarter, be stronger, and *win*.

Hal soon found that he didn't have to be tall to be smart, and in sports he was able to compensate for his size with a ferocious will and an unexpected ability to run very fast. He earned a scholarship to college, and after graduating, joined a large textile firm. The president of the firm, a man very much like himself, recognized a kindred spirit and took Hal under his wing. Despite the man's kindness to him, Hal didn't hesitate to take over his position. Since Hal had to appear rigidly moral in his own eyes, he justified his act by telling himself the man was too old and "it was in the best interests of the company"— a line he was to use again and again as he eliminated competitors.

Meanwhile he had married a girl he'd met in college. Like him, she was a Phi Beta Kappa, and he had initially admired her gregariousness, so unlike his own controlled behavior. But like most Hawks, his need to control her and assert his superiority over her won out. To fulfill his dream of what success meant, he insisted that they move to an expensive suburb where she was increasingly cut off from her family, her friends and any chance to begin a career. Bored and almost totally isolated, she began to drink. Her drinking gave him the justification he needed to spend more and more time at work and to seek com-

panionship elsewhere. He had many affairs, always with
women in his company whom he could impress with his
power. Some of these women fell in love with him, but he
never believed this. If they cared for him, he felt, there
must be something wrong with them, so he "punished"
them or increased his demands upon them until they
finally rejected him, just as he had expected them to all
along.

Hawks are not easily helped. Their compulsion to run
things and to be right gets in their way, and their defenses
are tough to break down. Hal also had the very real problem of living in a society that puts a false emphasis on
tallness. In addition, he was afraid that if he allowed
himself to be vulnerable, it would interfere with his business success, and others would take advantage of him. He
was only dimly aware of the hurt and pain and the contempt for himself his often ruthless behavior concealed.

Hal's first real breakthrough occurred when I asked him
if he had ever felt compassion for the child he'd been.
Suddenly he said, "You know, when I was a kid I used to
look up at the adults around me and think, I can't wait
to be big, the way they are—and then when I grew up,
I still had to look up. Do you know how that makes me
feel?" To his embarrassment, tears came to his eyes, and
he could not go on talking. For the first time in years he
had allowed some feeling for himself to emerge.

It was a beginning, and from there he was able to let
out some of his buried hurts and humiliations, and to
recognize that he was punishing his wife and his business
subordinates for wrongs done to him long before. And in
so doing, he himself was punished with a life devoid of joy
and love or any satisfaction save that of work.

To help his wife, and to help himself have a richer,
fuller life, Hal would have to let go and allow himself to
feel, would have to learn to forgive those who hurt him
and above all, himself, for being less than perfect.

Four

Mix and
Match

Dove-Ostrich, Dove-Hawk, Hawk-Hawk, Ostrich-Ostrich: which is the best combination? How, after you've identified your own pattern, do you choose—or consider—a potential partner?

In our society Dove-Hawk—a woman who is a Dove; a man, a Hawk—is probably the most common pairing. Dove (female)-Ostrich (male) is a close second. For many years women have been told from infancy that Dove-like behavior is the feminine ideal and that Hawkish behavior is the province of the male. These role lines are beginning to blur a bit today, but little girls are still being given dolls, toy ironing boards and carpet sweepers, and little boys fishing rods and baseball bats, in spite of psychologists' warnings of the dangers inherent in these forced attitudes.

We have also borrowed many of our models from old movies. Humphrey Bogart played Hawk to any number of Doves through the years, as did Jimmy Cagney, Clark Gable and John Wayne. It was only occasionally that such "heroes" tangled with their female counterparts.

In the Ostrich category Cary Grant was probably the

most charming, and Errol Flynn may have been the busiest, but both usually succumbed to Doves in the end. Even Garbo, the quintessential Ostrich, was not allowed to remain detached. Before the movie was over, some domineering Hawk firmly pointed her at least toward the altar.

Of course, role reversal was not entirely absent in movies of the past. Rosalind Russell and Joan Crawford frequently played Hawks, but they weren't entirely happy about their situation and in the end a manly Hawk "made a woman out of them." The only female Hawk who never succumbed is Mae West (still going strong today), and few think of her as "unwomanly." In films as in fantasies, all sorts of couples walk happily into the sunset together. In real life, some combinations of people work better than others. What follows are some "mix and matches" to consider before you marry again. They are of course only models to help you evaluate your situation. They do not indicate inevitable, incompatible *or* perfect couplings. As with the categories of Dove, Hawk and Ostrich themselves, these "matches" are described to help you recognize the characteristics of your own relationships.

Dove-Hawk

This could be called the archetypal "couple." It's Walter and Maude, from *Maude*, and reversed, it's Archie and Edith Bunker, from *All in the Family*. It's the strong and the weak, the *macho* and the mouse, the shrew and the milquetoast. It's every Dove's dream and downfall, and every Hawk's disappointment.

The Hawk may enter into this pairing believing that a gentle Dove is ideal, but the relationship is so *easy*, and finally, so boring, that the Hawk may soon be out looking for someone a little more mettlesome. Although Hawks demand adoration and obedience, they can't help feeling contempt for the person who supplies it.

The Dove has entered the relationship determined to

demonstrate perfect understanding and absolute devotion. To find that's not enough is a terrible blow.

DOVE (LOVER)-HAWK (INTELLECTUAL) : CASE HISTORY

Charles, a Hawk Intellectual, had waited until he was forty to marry. He had been searching for a Dove to dominate, but not just any Dove. She had to be worthy of him, his intellectual equal. He found what he was looking for in Sarah, a gravely sweet and successful poet with an international reputation in the world of letters. Sarah was tall, big-boned and plain, and her doubts about her appeal as a woman and her gentle nature had made her a Dove Lover, a person eager to give her all to love. Demanding and brilliant, Charles simply swept her off her feet—to live happily ever after.

"Ever after," for Sarah, was all too brief. Charles loved her in his Hawk fashion, but was compelled to prove that he was superior intellectually. He put her down constantly—even mocked her poems in front of her fellow writers. He did this compulsively, although privately he admired her work and respected her talent. He had, after all, married her for it.

Analysis

Sarah was accustomed to paying a price for love. She had learned early that she had to compensate for not being pretty, as her mother was. Her father had been kind to her in an absent-minded way, but he was rarely at home, and writing poetry had become her refuge in an otherwise lonely girlhood. She had never thought about marriage, believing herself too ugly. When Charles proposed, she was overwhelmed and grateful. She had achieved what her mother had told her was impossible for her—getting a husband.

Charles had also grown up as a loner. His parents were

totally absorbed in their work as physicians, and Charles was left to find his own way. In school he was the class "brain," winning prizes and honors far more easily than he won attention at home. His parents took it for granted their son was smart. Why wouldn't he be, with them as parents? So Charles never got what he was looking for—applause where it counted—at home. He believed he had failed, but that if he tried hard, he would find a way to win their love, to make them notice him. Since he never did, he was left with a great hunger, and an even greater doubt about how smart he really was.

Prognosis

This marriage couldn't be called happy, but it will probably last forever, as long as both partners remain fixed in their present attitudes. Sarah has seen the insecure child behind Charles's sneering façade, and her lover's love has turned to mother's love. She forgives him everything for having proven to the world that she is desirable as a woman. By not telling Charles what she feels, she does the one thing guaranteed to hold him. She smiles and says nothing, and keeps him feeling that he has not quite won—yet.

Ostrich-Ostrich

Ostriches in tandem may seem improbable, but actually, they might make a perfect pair. They may see each other only when entering and going out of the door; they may meet each other chiefly at parties; but they could have a lifetime of separate togetherness—pursuing their own interests, their own way.

Ostrich couples often have an understanding: "You go your way, I go mine." As long as neither partner goes too far or gets taken over by a Hawk or a Dove, they may live to celebrate their fiftieth wedding anniversary.

An O-O marriage could be a whirl of activity, desperately quiet resignation in front of a television screen, or a marriage of minds in academia. But all things considered, probably only an Ostrich could long tolerate another Ostrich.

OSTRICH-OSTRICH TUNE-OUTS: CASE HISTORY

George and Betty were a matched pair, two Tune-Outs who seemed to have a lot going for their marriage: a lovely home, nice children, individual hobbies and shared enthusiasm for camping. Where better to be together and apart at the same time than in a tent with two children? Communication about feelings, apart from complaints about the weather or the mosquitoes, is impossible in such a setting, as is satisfying sex.

After twenty years of this peaceful marriage, a lady Hawk decided George was fair game and lured him away. Betty came to me in genuine confusion.

"I thought we were so happy. Why would he do that? What could he possibly want?"

Had she ever asked him what he wanted?

"No."

Were they ever able to talk together about their feelings?

"Not often."

Had their sex life been good?

"Not really."

Betty had always told herself that if George wanted to discuss his feelings or their sex life, he would start the conversation. Since he didn't she felt it was better not to say anything. It might upset him. She also told me that early in their marriage she had left George briefly for another man, but it hadn't worked out and she had asked to come back. George had agreed and they had continued their life exactly as though they had never separated. Incredibly, they never once discussed her leaving or the reasons for it.

Several weeks after our session she came to tell me that George had asked to come back to *her* and *she* had agreed.

Had they discussed his leaving?

"No."

Analysis

George and Betty had both had the life crushed out of them at an early age. Although their backgrounds were different, the dynamics were similar, in that they both experienced neglect—one through benevolence and the other through overprotectiveness.

George's parents were free spirits who didn't believe in hampering a child. He was never disciplined, had no rules to follow and was given no direction. This permissiveness frightened him. He read it (quite accurately) as not caring.

"The kids whose parents loved them always had to be home by a specific time or they'd be punished. I could come in anytime. I used to pretend I had to leave a party like the others so they wouldn't know the truth about my folks."

George learned to affect an "I don't care" attitude to conceal his hurt and bewilderment, and gradually it became so much a part of him that he believed he really didn't care too much one way or the other about anything. He was left in a state of mild depression that passed for normal. His brief fling during marriage was a last attempt to come to life, but it required too much of him.

Betty's crushing was more direct. Her parents were worriers. They worried that Betty would get a cold and die of pneumonia, that she wouldn't pass her courses, that she'd lose her job, that she'd never get married. Since worry was the only emotion they showed freely, Betty grew up convinced that the world was a dangerous place and that she couldn't expect much of herself. George's calm (resignation) appealed to her after a life spent in the turmoil of tempests in teapots, but by then her spirit was nearly broken.

No one was more surprised than Betty when she became infatuated with a young man and attempted to leave George. This half-hearted attempt to break out proved too frightening, and she was grateful to be taken back.

Neither George nor Betty wanted to go into their problems in any depth, or to find out what was under their temporary rebellions. When Betty came to me it was to justify her feelings, not to examine or change them. When George returned, as she unconsciously knew he would, she had no further need for help.

Prognosis

The sex life of this couple will undoubtedly remain poor, and their communication nil. But unless one of them goes through a mid-life crisis and begins to question what they might have missed, the prognosis for their remaining together is good.

Dove-Ostrich

This pairing is usually based upon a mutual misunderstanding. The Dove in the first glow of love sees the Ostrich as strong and silent (someone to lean on) or reserved and well-mannered (someone who will help socially or in a career). The Ostrich, flushed out of hiding by passion, believes that loving attention would be wonderful for a change.

Then two people will be lucky to hang on to these illusions through the honeymoon, by which time the Ostrich will appear to the Dove as silent and stupid or as cold and frigid. Dove Loving will be seen now as stifling. The Ostrich will become bored by all that attention and retreat, and the Dove will react with bewilderment and wounded feelings.

There is some hope, however. Ostriches *can* be reached through sex, and if the Dove can keep fanning the sexual flames and learn to stay out of other areas, the Ostrich may relax.

All in all, this kind of relationship works better for the Ostrich than for the Dove. However, the Dove can take solace in the fact that he/she will actually have a lot of freedom to develop before the Ostrich will notice any change.

DOVE (GIVER) -OSTRICH (LOVER) : CASE HISTORY

Paul was a "chaser," an Ostrich Lover extraordinaire. Every woman he met was a target, and with his good looks, he had little trouble "scoring." He had been married for twenty years to Francis, and prefaced every affair with a firm statement of his intention never to leave his wife— just so there wouldn't be any doubt that this fling would be a temporary one. As a gynecologist, he had little trouble meeting women and having as many affairs as he had time for.

Francis, meantime, with a husband rarely at home, had little to give her Dove Love to. She knitted, wrote letters to her school chums and had seen the forty-first rerun of *I Love Lucy.*

It would seem that such an arrangement could go on forever. But Paul met his Waterloo, a stunning Ostrich Flirt, and fell head over heels in love with his own reflection.

Analysis

Paul's many affairs never completely convinced him that he was what the women he made love to believed he was. He pursued new women with the fervor born of desperation, and each time he sold himself to them, he sold himself to himself. Standing over his shoulder was the cool judgment of his father, who would have looked at his triumphs with distaste, as he had always looked at everything Paul did. Paul had worshiped his father, a prominent doctor, and had done everything in his power to please him. Medical school had not been his idea, but his father's. Even marrying Francis had been at his father's suggestion.

Paul believed he could never measure up to his father, who remained in his eyes "a man," as he was forever a boy. Out of this painful love for his father, all love became a thing to be avoided, to run away from.

That he fell in love with another Ostrich was not an accident: she, like his father, didn't succumb. That her rejection and his father's were due to entirely different reasons made no difference. Logic is not an issue when one is blindly following a pattern. Should he marry his Ostrich he will be in for deep disappointment. Francis gave him a stability he will be lost without.

Francis, who came from a working-class family, had married Paul because she thought he was handsome and romantic, and because he seemed to offer her a life of constant excitement: he would lead her, bring her out of herself, and some of his gaiety and charm would rub off on her. Her mother died when she was young, and Francis took care of her brothers and sister almost full time. She had little time to have friends or to date, or to develop any particular skills. Paul's proposal was such a miracle to her that after their marriage, she willingly waited for him and closed her eyes to his affairs, grateful to be allowed to stay in his life.

In the few years preceding Paul's big infatuation, Francis had grown increasingly unhappy and chided herself for it. She had all of the material things, and only *she* was his wife. When Paul said he would leave, she was at first numbed. Then some of the spunk she'd once had when she single-handedly ran her home after her mother's death came out and she began to fight to save herself.

Prognosis

Not good for the marriage, but hopeful for each of them. It won't hurt Paul to learn that women can also make demands, and that his new amour will never be there to come home to.

As for Francis, she will have to finally leave her television set and do some serious thinking about why she put up with this situation for so long. It could be the best thing that ever happened to her.

Dove-Dove

You might think this has to be the ideal combination. Two loving, giving people, eternally loving and giving. And it might occasionally work out that way. The catch is that Doves are rarely sexually attracted to each other. And it's hard to lose yourself in someone who's trying to lose themselves in you. Also, a true Dove knows better than anyone else about the time bomb buried under all that sweetness; they've been listening to their own tick for years.

However, D-D marriages frequently do last, even if for the wrong reasons, by making a mutual-dependency pact or forming what is known as a symbiotic relationship. It's "We'll cling to each other because if we don't, we'll both drown." This isn't good for either partner, and should a big wave come along, there is always the danger that one partner will decide to swim for it and leave the other to drown.

Even the fights may tend to be dull. How can there be any fireworks when each Dove is determined to take the blame? But all things considered, a D-D marriage is probably the best bet for the Dove who plans to stay that way. Certainly it's the safest.

DOVE (SUFFERER) -DOVE (GIVER) : CASE HISTORY

Alex and Julie were both gentle, undemanding Doves. They never fought, much less disagreed. True, Julie suffered from severe headaches that seemed to have no medical basis, but Alex was only too eager to take care of her.

Julie also suffered from guilt at the trouble her headaches caused "dear Alex." When the doctor suggested the problem might be mental rather than physical, she was terrified but brave. She sought help. Anything for Alex.

Alex, though devastated to think that his love hadn't been enough, also took the blow courageously. He gave up his bowling club and his theater group to devote himself full time to Julie's welfare.

Analysis

Alex had been a shy, sensitive boy with three large boisterous older brothers just like his father, who frightened Alex and gave his mother headaches. Alex became his mother's "best friend," and while he waited on her and took care of her, she protected him from his father and brothers. He learned to equate loving with giving, and because he felt safe in this role, he wanted it to continue in his marriage. He thought he had found someone like his mother in Julie, someone gentle and loving whom he could take care of.

Julie had been a quiet, obedient child, also unusually close to her mother. She thought of her mother as someone who'd "had a hard time in life, but who remained a saint." She was frightened of her father, though she secretly admired him. Her mother had taught her that to be a good wife, a woman must alway "give in" to her husband. Men were strong and domineering like Judy's father, but they were the breadwinners and should be catered to. So Julie married someone like her mother because she felt "safe," but really she wanted and expected a husband to be a demanding man like her father to whom she could surrender.

When Alex was unable to fill this role, she began, unconsciously, to feel anger. Since her Dove nature would not allow an expression of open hostility, she had headaches. To recover, she had to see that her secret demands of Alex were unreasonable; that the qualities she had loved in him from the beginning were still there. Since Julie had wanted only to learn the cause of her headaches, with this knowledge her suffering was alleviated and she discontinued treatment.

Prognosis

Good, as long as each of them remains comfortable within this limited framework.

Hawk-Ostrich

This combination has to be disastrous for both parties. Hawks must have someone to bully, but to find an Ostrich may take some doing. It will be a little like trying to catch smoke.

The Ostrich will find Hawks of any stripe simply too "heavy." Although a Hawk Hero might have a certain magnetism for an Ostrich Lover, the latter's attention span isn't too long and by the time the Hero gets his campaign into gear, his prey may have gone to greener pastures.

These pitfalls notwithstanding, there are a fair number of H-O marriages around. That angry man with the glaring eyes who just dragged his wife off the dance floor, the furious lady filling glasses at the punch bowl while her husband plays the life of the party are two. So if you're a Hawk or an Ostrich, take your cue. Better keep hunting or keep running—to another type.

HAWK (LOVER)-OSTRICH (ADDICT) : CASE HISTORY

Stacy was a Hawk Lover who had breezed through many affairs before marrying. She chose her men, won them, took them over, rearranged their lives, then dropped them contemptuously and moved on. She had always directed the show and brought down the curtain, so in her eyes, her affairs were never failures. But when she decided to marry Jake, an Ostrich Addict, all her wit and charm and drive came up against the brick wall of alcoholism.

The more she pumped her own brand of Hawk Love into him, the more inviting to him oblivion became. The "quick one before I go home for dinner" became five or six, and then all-night binges. To Jake, d.t.'s were less of a threat than Hawk Love.

Always before with men, Stacy had used the threat of withdrawal to maintain control and get her own way, but "How can you threaten someone who is too drunk to know what you're saying?" She hated to admit this defeat, particularly when the victor seemed to be a bottle, but for the first time in her life, she was at a loss.

Analysis

Stacy was the classic spoiled only child of upper-middle-class parents who gave in to her every demand. Like many spoiled children, she was not a little frightened of her seeming omnipotence. If *she* could control her parents, it meant she was on her own, virtually parentless. This scared her, but made her resolve to be as unlike them as possible. As she grew older, every relationship became a test for her. As long as someone stood up to her, she stayed. As soon as they gave in, she left with the same feelings of contempt for their weakness that she had felt for her parents.

Jake had been a real challenge to her during their courtship. He mocked her when she ordered him around and laughed at her tantrums. She thought that at last she had found a "parent" who could control her.

Actually, the healthy adult in Stacy didn't really want a parent, so there was constant conflict between this healthy adult side and the spoiled child that remained terrified of finding herself alone and in charge. The child in her looked for a parent substitute, and the adult made sure she chose badly because she knew she could really take care of herself now.

Jake, an extreme Ostrich, as addicts always are, was really drawn to the willfulness and bossiness he teased her about. Though he wouldn't admit it, he thought she would keep him straight. He was unaware of the panic behind her flamboyance and took her at her face value.

Jake had also been coddled as a child. His father had deserted his mother when Jake was a very young boy, so Jake became son-lover-husband to his mother.

When he was fourteen he "borrowed" a neighbor's car for a joy ride and accidentally hit an old man. It was not entirely his fault, but his guilt was enormous. His mother somehow got him out of it, just as she got him out of every bad scrape he managed to get into. He became dependent on being taken care of, and at the same time he was deeply disturbed by his role as "mother's sweetheart." His careless, mocking manner hid a frightened, insecure little boy deserted by his father and forced by his mother to be a man too soon.

Prognosis

Like most Hawks and Ostriches, Stacy and Jake were an interesting mix but a bad match. Attack and retreat are not patterns that lead to closeness and their relationship will either end or continue to cause each of them great suffering.

Hawk-Hawk

Like George and Martha in *Who's Afraid of Virginia Woolf?*, two Hawks may stay together because they get a perverse satisfaction out of the struggle. Two birds of prey, neither one can stand to lose, neither can afford to appear weak—and neither will give up.

Hawks don't often find other Hawks attractive. That's why so many go dressed in Dove feathers—at least until they have made their catch—when it's every Hawk for him/herself.

Hawks are prone to marry the same Hawk—twice. This is understandable. They don't like to give up in anything— and maybe the second time, they'll finally prove who's boss.

HAWK (AVENGER) -HAWK (AVENGER) : CASE HISTORY

It could be said that Arthur and Edith deserved each other. No one else would put up with either one of them. Theirs is not so much a marriage as a contest. Who will outsmart, outtalk, outthink the other first? Edith is a designer and Arthur a dress manufacturer, and as long as they stayed in their respective fields, the battles were conducted only from dinner to bedtime (their sex life was surprisingly good). When they decided to combine their talents and form a business partnership, it became a full-scale war. Customers were never sure whether they would be shown the new fall line or wind up under the tables dodging flying objects and pretending they hadn't heard what they had just heard.

Edith swears she wants to leave and Arthur says he'd be happy to pack her bags. But they have their assets and a lot of their lives tied up in the business now, so they have to find some way to salvage the marriage. Neither is willing to give way in any area or to consider changing. Both believe the other is at fault.

Analysis

Both being Hawks would seem trouble enough, but Edith's and Arthur's problems are compounded by each of them following patterns that are totally at cross-purposes. In Edith's home her mother was in charge, handling the money, setting the rules and commanding respect—or else. Arthur's father ruled in his home and made it clear that women were to be looked upon as necessary to men, but never equal. That Arthur and Edith married was due entirely to their strong physical attraction for each other. They both thought, in the beginning, that they'd work out the "who's boss" question later, and each secretly expected to be the victor.

Their exclusively Hawk responses to life came out of the same climate. They had both had to fight for their goals. Neither had been loved for simply being, but had felt the need to be "somebody" almost from birth. Naturally, they carried this "I'll show the world" attitude into their marriage.

Prognosis

Not necessarily bad. Despite the fights, these two are still physically drawn to each other, and respect each other's abilities professionally. But for the marriage to continue, they will have to call a truce long enough to get to know the other sides of themselves and of each other.

What can you do after you have identified yourself and a potential partner in these matches? There are positive steps you can take to make a relationship work. If you are in love with . . .

a *Dove*, you can:
1. Encourage your Dove to be assertive, by not putting him/her down when they try.

2. Refuse to make decisions for your partner, even if you enjoy being in charge.

3. Understand the panic beneath your Dove's docility or excessive giving. However unrealistic the fear, Doves are afraid you will leave them.

4. Be aware of the unexpressed anger beneath their Dove façade and encourage them to express it by showing them that you will still love them when they do.

5. Show them that you love their gentleness and ability to give. After all, you were drawn to it originally.

an *Ostrich*, you can:

1. Encourage your partner to reveal feelings to you by letting him/her know that you won't betray those feelings by using them as a weapon in your next argument.

2. Make a point of showing pride in your ability to express feelings, and show that you will take the same pride in him/her if they follow suit.

3. Don't smother. Respect your Ostrich's deep need for privacy. Stand back and give him/her plenty of space to come and go. Your Ostrich will lose his/her fear and love you more.

4. Realize that your Ostrich is probably sensitive and possibly shy, and may need more support than you think—but remember, sudden moves may trigger flight.

5. Try to express your needs without making them sound as if they were commands.

a *Hawk*, you can:

1. Stand up for what you genuinely believe in. Your Hawk may believe he/she wants you to be submissive, but eventually he/she will feel contempt for your weakness.

2. Always show that you love your Hawk—even when you are being firm.

3. Remember the Hawk's demand that you be perfect is based on fear of his/her own imagined imperfections. Since your Hawk believes he/she must be perfect, so must those who "belong" to him/her.

4. Be able to give in occasionally, knowing how much the Hawk has invested in pride.

5. Don't get into the "who's boss?" debate.

6. Encourage your partner to see that his/her "mistakes" are *not* so terrible by showing him/her you love him/her even more for being human.

Part Two

Change Your Pattern

Five

Stand Up to Your Voices

C AN you stop giving, suffering and loving in a way that wipes you out?

Can you stop running around that same sad circle of loneliness?

Can you stop your relentless pursuit of success or perfection or getting even?

I think you can.

It may seem easier to change partners than to change the patterns of behavior that you've followed since you can remember, but in the long run it doesn't work. A new partner may change the dynamics of your problems, but you'll soon find yourself right back in the same old ruts, and this time the terror of making another mistake may be paralyzing.

The answer, of course, is to change yourself. You have examined the Pattern Principle, determined the behavior patterns causing you difficulties, and now must begin the work of changing.

The next three chapters will deal with how to:

Listen to the voices directing your behavior
Unravel your past to understand the whys of your behavior
Take action with exercises designed to change your behavior

One of the first questions I ask people who are having difficulty adjusting to change, particularly after a divorce, is: "What do your inner voices say?" And do you stand up to them when they "put you down"?

The first reaction is usually an embarrassed laugh and an incredulous "Voices?"

But invariably, if they listen, they hear the voices. So will you. Everyone has them, but they go on in your head with such incredible swiftness and are lodged so deep within you that you are seldom fully aware of them. These unsummoned ghosts of your past are constantly chastising, cheering, exhorting, warning, goading, instructing—and sometimes torturing you. You may call them your conscience, but more accurately, they are the remembered voices of your parents, your teachers, your friends, your enemies. (The loudest are usually those of your parents because they were the most important to you.)

Sometimes the clamor of your voices is deafening. Frequently they are contradictory. Their message can be positive and helpful, but far too often they are destructive. Various psychiatrists have described these inner voices: Thomas A. Harris in Chapter 2, "Parent-Adult-Child," *I'm OK, You're OK* (Harper & Row, 1969), and Dr. Theodore I. Rubin in *Compassion and Self-Hate* (McKay, 1975).

Here is a sample of an "inner dialogue" given to me by a client when I asked him to sit still and to listen: "What are you doing sitting here? Are you crazy? Voices! Ridiculous. You should be doing something worthwhile. You forgot to pay the electric bill last month. Last night you left the record player on. Careless. This is stupid. I don't know why anyone would imagine I had voices. People will think I am crazy. They do anyhow. Don't think about that. I'm getting a headache. I'm not going to sit here any longer. See there, so shallow you can't even sit still and think for five minutes."

To hear your voices, stop after you read this paragraph and try a simple experiment. Sit still, close your eyes and make no effort to control your thoughts. After three minutes, open your eyes and write down what you heard.

Then identify the voice. Is it really your own? Does it sound familiar? What was the tone; supportive, critical, angry, impatient, rushed, quiet? Was it a loud voice or soft? Who used to say those things to you? Your mother or father? And did you believe them then? Probably—you were small and young and they were in authority, they *must* know. But did they? And were you really so bad?

You may say, "But they can't hurt me now. I left home years ago." True. But what you have done is to internalize their voices. They have become your own now—and you are being put down by ghosts who should no longer have any power over you and who were not always right when they did.

Many people find their voices particularly harsh when they try to do something positive for themselves. Here is dialogue from a writer who was assaulted every time she sat down to write:

"I can't write today. I'm just too tired. Tired! From what? I can't write anyway . . . everything I write is a cliché. Why does everybody else do it so easily? Everything has already been said. God, I'm tired. Your problem is, you're just lazy. You're the laziest human being who ever lived, you'll never amount to anything. But I'm so tired . . . lazy!"

How do you stop these negative voices? First make yourself aware of them, then literally tell them to shut up. To get lost. To leave you alone. Or by a quiet statement, "No, that's not true. I am *not* lazy. I *am* tired" (and no wonder, with a battle of this magnitude going on in your head).

Like mastering anything, learning to fight back by telling these voices to be still takes time, desire, patience and repetition. But it can be done.

Once you are aware of what's going on, you will be better able to deal with your voices when you find you are using them against yourself.

One woman told me that she startled everyone around her and herself by answering her voices out loud in the middle of a church service. She had been trying to pray when her most nagging voice began inside her head, "Look at you trying to pray. What a hypocrite. You shouldn't even be here. You are terrible . . ." and on and on, pointing out her every mistake during the past week with a viciousness that would have been beneath her worst enemy. This realization struck her so forcibly that she spoke out loud: "But what have I done that is so terrible?"

She later told me, "No professional torturer could hit my vulnerable spots so accurately, and I was just taking it, one tongue-lashing after another, as though I were a criminal."

Some people feel they need to be told what an awful person they are in order to keep themselves humble or to make them do the things they would rather avoid, or they believe they would get nothing at all done without this internal nagging.

This is simply not true. These verbal whippings are debilitating. They block creativity and it would be possible to accomplish more without them. They are also demoralizing. And so often, what is accomplished gives little real satisfaction as a result of these nagging voices.

A writer described it this way: "It's as if I have a huge bulldog inside me that is perpetually hungry. It growls constantly and I feed it with my accomplishments. An article, say, will keep it quiet for a few days. Once I wrote

an entire book. That was a big meal and the dog gnawed
contentedly on the bones for nearly a month. It was the
first peace I'd had in years. Then it started again, nipping
at my heels, howling at night . . . it's like a giant maw that
will never, never be filled." His allusion to "maw" was
not accidental. His "maw" (mother) had pushed him in-
terminably and he had obviously internalized her voice.

A woman described a similar experience this way: "I'm
only at peace when I'm pregnant. Then I can say to my
voices, 'Leave me alone. I'm doing something important.'
And it lasts until the baby is about a month old and then—
boom!—they are off again, telling me what a flop I am."

Susan, a successful and driven lawyer who disbelieved
what I was telling her about her own voices, had a telephone conversation with her mother one day and suddenly understood both her voices and their source. She had
had an incredible week, won a law case, signed an important new client, been praised by a judge for a brilliant
defense. She called her mother to tell her the news. Her
mother's response was, "That's nice, darling." Long pause.
"What are you doing Saturday night? Going out, I hope."

Susan said, "For a second I was dumfounded. Saturday
night? But what— Then I got it. All the blood rushed to
my head and I couldn't breathe! She was telling me, 'You
may have a career but you don't have a date for Saturday
night. You're not a successful woman—nobody wants
you.' "

Susan realized her mother had been saying variations of
this for years: when she brought home A's but didn't get
the most valentines; when she'd just had her hair set in
a new way and her mother would look at her silently for
a long time and then say, "Did you notice Mary Tyler
Moore's hair on Saturday night? Now, *she* knows what to
do with her hair. So attractive."

Now, in none of these instances had her mother criticized
her outright, but the implication was there. This successful

attorney was not meeting her mother's standards and she never would, because the standards changed from day to day. Curiously, when she did get serious about a young man during law school, her mother shifted ground and suggested that her grades would fall behind if she became too involved with him. The message she got was clear, however. She wasn't good enough. Nothing she did would ever be good enough. Even if she had done what her mother was subliminally suggesting to her—have dates, get married, have children—her mother would, of course, have said, when she called to report the baby's first tooth, "That's nice, dear, but I remember when you used to tell me about your law cases and *important* things."

Susan's mother, in this case, probably has her *own* demons to contend with, and undoubtedly is more than a little jealous of her daughter and totally unaware of the havoc she has created. Were she taken to task, she would defend herself furiously: she was only thinking of her daughter's happiness. Small wonder that Susan had internalized her mother's voice and was tyrannized by it.

Without realizing it, Susan had used her mother's "voice" for years to keep herself in check. She was afraid:

Of getting "too big for her britches"
Of being like her mother
Of not being like her mother (and staying unmarried)
Of daring to become as "big" as she secretly felt she was capable of becoming
Of failing abysmally
Of incurring more of her mother's taunts if she failed
Of having to listen to her mother's innuendos if she succeeded but didn't get married

Keeping the voices alive kept Susan only half alive, but she believed that if she silenced them she would "kill" her mother symbolically. Then she would be "alone, cut off and rudderless, with no one to guide me." Since she thought she would be abandoned if she dared to strike out on her own, she had a great deal at stake in not believing that she had voices.

Exercise

Sit alone in a room, close your eyes and listen. Three minutes the first day, five the second, ten the third. Write down what you hear. Try to identify the voice. Answer the voice as firmly and positively as possible whenever the message to you is a negative one, or one that no longer applies to your present circumstances.

Six

Do-It-Yourself Unraveling

U NLESS you've taken the time to find out who you really are and what you require in another person, you'll probably fall in love with the first "warm body" that responds to you after your divorce or separation. This may alleviate your pain or divert you from it, but it may also put you back into a relationship very similar to the one just ended.

To avoid such a repetition, in any consideration of remarriage or in beginning a new relationship, you must be able to answer the question "What makes me think this relationship will be more successful than the last one?"

Several writers in the field of post-divorce adjustment have emphasized the need for self-analysis. William J. Goode, in *After Divorce* (Free Press, 1956), recognized the need for "unraveling of marital habits" in response to the trauma of divorce. Ten years later Morton M. Hunt advocated "divorce work" to alleviate "role disturbance," including tears, reflection and talk to discharge feelings and slowly modify one's habits and expectations in order to establish a new life (*The World of the Formerly Married*, McGraw-Hill).

The material that follows is a practical guide to self-unraveling. The goal of do-it-yourself unraveling should not be an all-encompassing renovation of yourself. Rather, the process allows you to confront yourself honestly, to examine the details of your life and integrate these insights in order to modify your behavior and face your future with more self-understanding.

Unraveling must move along three lines. The first is to discover the person you brought to your first marriage: what you were as a result of your early years, your relationship with your parents and siblings, and your early experiences. The second part focuses on the patterns you developed and your partner reinforced during your marriage or last serious relationship. The third line is to help you to find out what kind of person you are *now* and what you want from your future.

Unraveling is not an easy process. It takes courage to look back, but it is necessary to search the past for clues to the future if we are to stop rigidly repeating destructive patterns and learn to respond spontaneously to life.

Since our feelings about ourselves are very complex, the questions that follow may lead you into what psychologists call "free association." Most of us develop only a part of an idea at a time. This thought fragment can be allowed to ferment and develop or it can be totally lost. I suggest carrying a slip of paper and a pen with you at all times. If during the unraveling process a revelation occurs, scribble down a word or two that will evoke the same thought during the time you set aside for self-unraveling.

Feel free to pursue any line of thought that comes to your mind, and investigate fully any tangent you start to develop. After all, you are doing this analysis on your own and for yourself. If sexual variety is extremely important to your personal satisfaction, if you find living with another person claustrophobic, if you really want to quit your nice secure job and raise goats, this is the time to admit the facts to yourself and determine their implications for the failure of your marriage and the success of your future interpersonal encounters.

As your patterns begin to emerge, don't condemn yourself for them if they seem to have led to difficulties. Remember that as a child you formed these patterns because they promised you a measure of safety, or love, or some control over what might otherwise have seemed overwhelming obstacles.

The suggested outline for do-it-yourself unraveling is not intended to be all-inclusive. For instance, there is no mention of the importance of religion in your life or the kinds of people you choose as friends or how much you enjoy reading or going to the theater. Yet all of these questions are important and may be central to the personality of one individual or another. I hope the questions are general enough to lead you to an examination of your own specific interests.

As I have already noted, do-it-yourself unraveling is not for everyone. Some of us require professional counseling to overcome the crises engendered by divorce. Some can attempt self-analysis only as an adjunct to professional analysis and might use self-unraveling to sort out some feelings and prepare for clinical visits. However, if you have emerged from the initial shock of separation and worked through the emotional experiences provoked by it with a determination to face front and proceed forward, do-it-yourself unraveling is the next step in future growth whether you contemplate marriage for the first time, remarriage, forming a new relationship or remaining single.

Unraveling demands that you be absolutely honest in your responses. Write everything down so that you can be objective in your self-appraisal. This method will yield greater insights than would result from discussing your life with someone else—be it a friend or relative. Besides, you'll have a permanent account of yourself for future reference, penned by the one person who should know you best—you!

A few words of advice before you begin. First, take it easy. Unraveling is like exercising; you have to build to maximum effort slowly. You cannot sit down, pen in hand, questions before you, and decide to change your entire life instantly. It's impossible to alter old patterns overnight. What you need are small triumphs, workable insights that you can actually put into practice.

Be flexible so that one minor error in judgment will not slow your future progress. Keep in mind that any constructive motion is better than no motion at all.

Expect to hit some plateaus. A success may be followed by a failure. Most learning does not take place evenly.

Still, an I'll-work-on-it-later attitude is self-defeating and usually reflects an underlying fear of failure.

Remember the aims of unraveling:

Examine your early behavior patterns in dealing with others, particularly in close relationships.

Assess your strengths and weaknesses and define future goals according to your own, not society's, needs.

Pinpoint problem areas and attitudes that need special consideration.

Take constructive action that will make your next relationship more successful.

Before you go to work on the questions, here is a simple list of guidelines:

Set aside a *minimum* daily time for the process. I suggest forty-five minutes a day. Cover as much as you wish, and continue from where you left off the next day. Some days you may simply want to think about the questions and your answers.

Work in the same place every day; find a comfortable setting for the purpose.

Be willing to give extra time when required.

Learn how to "free" your mind. If a thought, however unrelated to the question, occurs, go with it. Write down exactly what comes to your mind with no editing, and follow it through to the next thought. You are then "free associating," and you'll find that your random thoughts will often lead back to the original question and that you may gain an insight on the way.

Stress feelings rather than just describing experiences.

Get a spiral or loose-leaf notebook in which to set down your thoughts.

After you have answered the questions that follow for yourself, try answering some of the key questions as your former mate would have, or if you have already found someone you would consider marrying, as you think he or she would. This might give you a clue about whether you are repeating your pattern.

I envision these three sets of questions ("Childhood," "Courtship and Marriage" and "Who Am I Now?") as a reference source as well as an immediate "plan of attack." Perhaps you'll want to recheck your changing feelings after you marry again, or verify your need to remain single, or analyze your approach to sexuality ten years from now. Certain aspects of your life will need repeated unraveling. And you may wish to devise supplementary questions of your own as you go along.

Some of the tests, questions or exercises may appear too difficult—or too easy. But *they work*.

Once you understand the principles of unraveling and see them work in your own life, you will realize that it is a lifelong process—one that is continually rewarding.

———◇———

Self-Analysis

Part 1—Childhood

WHAT EFFECTS DID MY HISTORY PRIOR TO MY FIRST MARRIAGE HAVE ON THAT MARRIAGE?

A. Review in detail of my preschool years.

1. What kind of person was my mother while I was growing up?
   a. Describe mother in detail.
   b. What was our relationship like?
2. What was my relationship with my father?
   a. Describe my father's personality traits in detail.
3. What was my relationship with my sisters and brothers?
   a. What did we argue about?
   b. How did I feel toward them?
4. Do I remember anything about my developmental landmarks in that period? (For example, when did I walk, sit, talk, discover sexual differences? What about toilet training, breast or bottle feeding? Was there anything memorable or significant during these occurrences that I know of?)
5. Who else was important in my preschool life? Aunts, uncles, grandparents, neighbors? How did I relate to them? They to me?
6. Did I have any physical problems or illnesses during this period?
7. Do I remember this time of my life with joy or pain?
   a. Is it difficult for me to remember anything at all?
   b. Can I think of any reasons why I may have blanked this period?
   c. Can I ask anyone for details that might bring it back?

8. Describe any significant or dramatic events that occured in my preschool years (illness, accidents, deaths in the family, punishments, rewards).

B. What were my school years like?

 1. How did I behave and perform in kindergarten? (Continue through last year of schooling.) Did I like teachers or dislike them generally? Does any pattern emerge in my attitude toward authority?
 2. What was my achievement in relationship to my innate intelligence?
     a. How do I judge this?
     b. How did I feel about myself in this regard?
 3. What did others in my family expect from me:
     a. Academically?
     b. In extracurricular activities—sports, clubs, societies?
 4. What did my friends think of me in terms of being smart or not smart?
 5. What kinds of friends did I have during high school?
     a. Describe my social life during this period.
     b. Did I believe I was popular? With own sex? With opposite sex?
     c. How did I feel about this?
 6. Did I plan for a career or further education after high school? How?
 7. What were my major talents? Interests?
 8. What were my family relationships like while I was in school?
     a. Who was the disciplinarian?
     b. How did my parents get along?
     c. With which parent or family member did I have the most rapport?
     d. How much support did my family give me in terms of school activities and homework?
 9. What did I think of myself physically?
     a. How did my family, parents, siblings, relatives react to my appearance?

    b. How did my peers react to me in terms of my attractiveness?

    c. When did I develop sexual interest and curiosity? How did I express this?

    d. How much physical contact took place in my home? Between parents and me? Between my parents?

10. What did I learn about sex from my parents?

11. How would I describe my personality during my school years?

12. What were my most significant relationships while in school?

C. What outside work experiences did I have during school years?

    1. Did my family require that I perform certain duties: dishes, lawn, errands, my room? How did I react?

D. What work experiences did I have after leaving school and before my marriage?

    1. What is my employment history?

    2. What jobs did I enjoy most? Or, what aspects of my various jobs did I enjoy most?

    3. What kind of social life did I have while working?

    4. How did my schooling and my job (s) relate to each other?

    5. Have I had dreams about my future which never materialized?

       a. Why didn't they "come true"?

    6. Did my social activities and relationships change after formal schooling? How?

E. What were my premarital social relationships like?

    1. List each relationship that I would consider more than casual. Describe my behavior in these relationships in detail.

    2. How did my family react to each of my relationships? What about my friends?

    3. How did I communicate during this period (verbally and nonverbally)?

4. Do I see similarities in the types of people I was attracted to?
5. How did I behave, generally, during my premarital dating period?
6. Did I regard every date as a potential marriage partner? If so, why?

Part 2—Courtship and Marriage

A. What first attracted me to my spouse?
  1. Was he/she similar to earlier attractions?
  2. If different, how?
B. How well did I know my spouse before we were married?
  1. How long was our courtship? Was it too long? Too short?
  2. Did we share many experiences, interests together during courtship?
  3. What character traits or behavior patterns did my spouse display before our marriage?
  4. How well did I evaluate him/her during courtship in light of my experience after marriage?
  5. How did I describe him/her to friends and family in the first glow of love?
  6. What character traits or behavior patterns changed after marriage?
  7. Evaluate spouse honestly before, during and after marriage.
  8. Were there traits I disliked but thought I could change after marriage?
C. How honest was I during courtship?
  1. Did I show my real self, or was I putting my best foot forward at all times?
  2. How did I change after marriage?
  3. Describe my feelings about myself before, during and after marriage.
D. Who instigated the idea of marriage?

1. Did I feel pressured into marriage by my family?
2. Were a lot of my friends getting married and did I feel I would be left out?
3. Did I feel certain that I wanted to marry?
   a. Did I believe our marriage was going to be successful?
4. Were we in agreement about marriage ceremony? Honeymoon?
   a. How did we both react?

E. Was there a strong physical attraction?

1. If there was sex before marriage:
   a. Was it accompanied by guilt?
   b. Was it satisfying?
2. How did this change after marriage?

F. Did we discuss living arrangements and finances before wedding?

1. Did we clarify our areas of individual responsibility beforehand?

G. When did the first snarl in our marriage appear?

1. Did we trust each other?
2. Did physical attraction grow or diminish?
3. Did my tolerance for certain habits change?

H. How well did we communicate?

1. Describe the communication between me and my ex-spouse during marriage.
   a. Did I feel free to speak openly? Did my ex? Did I express my real needs and wants?
   b. Did one of us often tune out the other?
   c. Did I resort to needling and negative remarks to get attention or to hurt? Did my ex?
2. Was there often a lack of communication or a misunderstanding or misinterpretation of each other's words or actions?
   a. Was there little to talk about because we lacked common interests?
   b. If so, how did I handle lack of communication?

3. Was I too passive in accepting hostile remarks from my spouse?

   a. Did he/she become accustomed to this reaction?

   b. What did this lead to in our relationship?

4. Did one of us threaten or belittle the other in much of our verbal intercourse?

I.   How well did we communicate nonverbally?

1. How much physical contact did we share in terms of touching (holding hands, embracing)?

2. Am I sensitive to being touched or touching?

   a. Did I communicate these feelings?

3. Did I encourage or obstruct physical contact?

J.   What was our sexual relationship like?

1. Did I make an effort to be stimulating?

2. How did I dress?

   a. How did I take care of myself?

   b. How did I encourage sexuality?

3. How did we communicate sexual interest to each other?

   a. What signals did I use? Were they picked up?

   b. What signals did my spouse use? How did I respond verbally? Nonverbally?

4. How did we get into love-making? Describe in some detail both verbal and nonverbal (touching, fondling, kissing, etc.) "lead-ins."

5. How much communication was there about intercourse?

   a. Did I share what I enjoyed and what I didn't?

   b. Did we try new sexual experiences together?

   c. Did I feel free to let my spouse know I wasn't "in the mood"?

   d. If my spouse indicated that he/she wasn't in the mood, did I feel unwanted?

   e. Did we exchange understandable signals so that

we both realized the other's stage of excitement and orgasm?

   f. Did we communicate after ejaculation or orgasm?

6. How much variety was there in our sexual relationship?

   a. Did I or my spouse lack creativity and energy during sex?

   b. Was our sex very routine in terms of position?

   c. Did we experience very routinized sex in terms of time, place?

   d. Was I relaxed enough so that we both felt free to act and react spontaneously? Was my ex?

K. How did we make decisions during our lives together?

1. Did we share decision making?

   a. Did we talk about how decisions were made?

   b. Did we divide decision making? How?

   c. Was I left out of the decision making?

   d. Did I want to give up a voice in decision making?

   e. Did I want more voice?

   f. What happened when there were disagreements about decisions? Did this occur frequently?

L. Did we share outside interests, activities?

1. What were my interests during marriage? What were my spouse's? What were common interests?

2. Did I show curiosity and respect for his/her independent interests? Did he/she for mine?

3. Were our interests so enmeshed that there was little room for individuality and growth?

4. How did our interests—common and independent—change from courtship through marriage to the point of divorce?

M. What was the economic situation of our marriage?

1. Did I overspend? Did he/she? Did we both?

2. Did we try to save money?

3. Were either of us too conservative?

4. Did we openly discuss economic problems and philosophies?
5. Were there real financial problems?
    a. Did I resent having too little money?
N. What kind of social life did we have?
 1. Did we try to build common social activities?
 2. Did either or both of us establish friendships outside of the home which supported our relationship?
 3. Did either of us socialize instead of honestly trying to bolster our failing relationship?
O. How did our families affect our marriage?
 1. Was there residual dependency on either of our immediate families that caused conflict throughout our marriage?
 2. Did I consider my spouse secondary to my mother, father, or even sister or brother?
 3. Did I experience difficulty in moving away from my family emotionally? Geographically?
 4. Did unscheduled family visits disrupt our home life?
    a. Cause fights?
    b. How did I react?
 5. Did other family members have a great deal of influence in our decision making?
P. Further analysis of the relationship.
 1. Did I feel sympathetic to my spouse when he/she was down or needed encouragement?
 2. Did I assume my mate's frame of reference or mood instead of staying in my own skin?
 3. How much time did I spend at home? How much did she/he?
 4. Did I become increasingly indifferent and blasé about our relationship as time went on?
 5. Was I willing to accept positive suggestions from my spouse?
 6. How did I react to criticism?
Q. If there were children, how did they affect marriage?

1. Did we have child to strengthen our marriage? If so, did it, in the beginning—or did it make the gulf wider?
2. Did either of us use the child or children against each other?
3. Did I feel I had too much responsibility for the children?

R. If there were no children, how did this affect marriage?
   a. Was this a choice?
   b. If so, was the decision a mutual one?
   c. How did I feel about this?

Part 3—Who Am I Now?

A. What kind of person am I now?
   1. What kinds of activities do I enjoy in general?
   2. What are my feelings about private time?
   3. What part does socializing play in my life?
      a. Do I depend solely on others for my satisfaction?
      b. Do I socialize as a means of getting away from myself?
      c. Do I withdraw from others when under stress?
   4. Do I enjoy sports activities?
      a. Am I a physical person who enjoys using my body?
      b. Do I plan activities for the out-of-doors?
      c. What is my energy level?
         1) Am I always tired?
         2) Am I restless with "extra" energy?
   5. Do I enjoy esthetic activities such as reading, sculpting, painting, going to museums and theaters?
   6. Do I prefer cognitive, intellectual, problem-solving pursuits?
   7. Are some of my most pleasurable and exciting times spent in daydreaming and fantasizing?
   8. Take the last week or two and write out a detailed description of significant activities and how they gratified or frustrated me.

B. What kind of activities do I enjoy in the home?

   1. How do I feel about domestic activities such as cooking, house-cleaning, repairing appliances, decorating, painting, etc.?

   2. Do I, or do I not, believe I would enjoy the responsibilities of children?

   3. If I am a woman, do I find running a home boring or rewarding?

   4. How do I feel about a woman's role in the home?

C. What holds the highest priority for me?

    a. Home life?

    b. Career?

D. What is my typical mood?

   1. Do I usually take the optimistic viewpoint, feeling that tomorrow will be better?

   2. Am I a pessimist assuming the worst will happen?

   3. Do I frequently experience depression—low energy, loss of sexual desire, gloom, suicidal thought, etc.?

   4. Am I often tense and easily upset? Do I have a low tolerance for frustration, failure?

E. Can I really give of myself to someone else?

   1. Do I experience a sense of satisfaction from pleasing others?

    a. Do I always have an ulterior motive for pleasing?

   2. Give specific examples of benevolence. Of withholding.

   3. On the sexual level, how important is my partner's satisfaction?

   4. Do I feel put upon if I give without receiving open appreciation in return?

   5. Do I resent giving gifts on formal occasions such as birthdays, weddings, etc.?

   6. Do I go overboard in buying gifts? Am I buying love?

   7. Do most of the relationships I enter into depend on how much the other person can offer me?

F. How do I react in tense or anxiety-producing situations?

(Most of us react in a variety of ways. Write out an example of a situation in which I reacted in any of the following ways):

1. Do I try to escape or pretend it never happened?
   a. How? By drinking too much, overeating, watching television, escape-reading, taking tranquilizers or sleeping pills?
2. Do I try to act cool, as if I am not feeling tension, and fool myself and others?
3. Do I try to place the blame for what is happening on others? Lash out at them verbally? Physically?
4. Do I have to force myself to socialize, be with others?
5. Do I try to compensate for what I consider my social deficits by trying to become very competent in another area?
6. Do I justify everything I do and make excuses for what I fail to do?
7. Do I throw myself into activities to overcome anxiety and a feeling of helplessness?
8. Do I refuse to deal with my emotions and intellectualize?
9. Do I pursue pleasure in order not to think about, act on or acknowledge important issues in my life?

G. How relaxed and playful can I be?

1. Is my tension level so high that I can't enjoy events that most people consider recreational?
2. How often do I set aside time during my day just to relax? Does anxiety interfere with my ability to do this?
3. Can I have fun without worrying about what others think of me?
   a. Do I feel guilty when having fun, when I'm not "producing"?
   b. Am I afraid that I will do something stupid or that some other weakness of mine will become obvious if I am not fully in control of my emotions in all situations?

c. Am I so self-conscious in situations that I can never "let loose"?

4. Do I ever do something that is "crazy" just for its own sake?

5. Do I need help to relax—such as alcohol or marijuana?

6. Do I tend to analyze everything I do or am going to do and thus prohibit spontaneity?

7. Am I always the life of the party? Do I love to be?

8. Do I feel as if I can never have enough fun? Is "here today, gone tomorrow" my philosophy?

9. Can I laugh easily at myself?

H. What do I think of my physical appearance?

1. Am I attractive to others? How am I sure of that?

a. Describe two parts of my body that are most appealing.

b. What are my feelings when someone refers to my physical attractiveness?

c. Do I enjoy being physically attractive to others?

2. Do most people consider me unattractive?

a. Describe two clear indications of this.

b. Describe the two most unappealing parts of my body.

3. What physical defects or weaknesses do I believe affect my relations with others?

4. How well do I take care of my body?

a. Do I allow myself to become careless about my appearance?

b. Do I pay much attention to my grooming? Dress? Current fashions?

c. Am I too fat? Too thin?

d. How does my cleanliness or lack of it affect sexual activity in my life?

5. Do I spend time with and enjoy myself as a physical person, for example, while bathing?

6. How sensitive am I to being seen in the nude by someone close to me?

7. What do I consider my physical assets and strong points?
   a. What do I do to accentuate these assets?

I. How much affection can I express openly?

1. Can I say warm, loving things to others? Do I?
2. Do I compliment others easily?
3. How comfortable am I when receiving compliments and affection from others?
4. Is it easy for me to touch others physically?
   a. Can I hug, kiss, hold easily?
   b. Do I *need* to touch constantly, want to be held?
   c. Do I hold hands, kiss, in public? Why?
5. How do I react when others touch me?
   a. How well do they have to know me before I feel comfortable?

J. How strong is my sexual drive?

1. Under what circumstances can I "take it or leave it"?
   a. What religious tenets affect my sexual impulses?
   b. Do I experience guilt feelings about sex?
   c. Do I feel that sexual activity leads to too much loss of self-control?
   d. Do I experience too much pleasure in sexual activity?
2. Do I believe I have excessive sexual needs?
   a. Do I require sexual activity on a daily basis? Several times daily?
3. Do I demand that my partner constantly prove his love sexually?
4. Does physical contact make me anxious?
5. Am I ashamed of nudity?
6. Can I communicate feelings of pleasure in sex to my partner, e.g., "That feels good!" "I like that"?
7. How much do I contribute to relationships of a sexual nature?
   a. Can I initiate a sexual encounter?
   b. Can I take an assertive role in intercourse?

8. How comfortable am I during sexual interaction?
9. How do I feel about autoerotic practices?

K. How intelligent am I?

1. Am I average, above average, below average, stupid, or exceptionally bright?
   a. What brought me to this conclusion?
2. How do I use my intelligence in social relationships?
3. Do I have to make certain that others *know* how smart I am?
4. Do I feel intellectually inferior to most other people and avoid situations which would make this obvious?
5. Do I avoid situations or activities which demand intellectual effort?
6. How do I use my mind in everyday activities? What value does this have for me?

L. Do I derive satisfaction out of the work that I do most of the week?

1. Is my career satisfying? In what ways?
2. Do I dread getting to work in the morning?
3. Do I dream of doing something other than what I am doing now?
4. Name three things that I might want to do differently in terms of my work or career.
5. What keeps me from following through with my career goals?
6. Have I ever tried to make plans for a job change?

M. What are my goals in life?

1. Am I going nowhere?
2. Is my life very structured?
3. Although my life goals may change, do I feel comfortable with what I am doing with my life now? Write a short paragraph on my purpose and how what I am doing does or does not satisfy this purpose.
4. What are my short-range goals? Are these consistent with my long-range goals?

5. Do I have difficulty determining what things are worth working for?

N. What is my philosophy of life?

1. What kinds of things do I feel I should be doing in this life?

2. What kinds of actions have I taken to implement this philosophy?

3. Are there times when my beliefs and my actions conflict?

4. Do I try to "get away with" doing things that I basically do not believe should be done? For example, I might have a religious feeling regarding a certain ritual but not follow through by actually performing the ritual because it is inconvenient, or cheat from a large corporation because "they can afford it."

5. What keeps me from following through with my philosophical goals?

Ledger

The use of a ledger is another excellent method of analyzing your behavior patterns and learning new ways of behavior.

The ledger allows you to record your behavior in given situations, past and present. It helps you recognize your underlying feelings in the situation and allows you to find more positive and satisfying ways of handling those situations.

Setting up a ledger is simple. Use the back or your self-analysis notebook. Open to a double-page spread. Across the top of the two pages, write the following topic headings and rule lines down the page where appropriate.

1. Current Experience
2. Underlying Feeling State
3. Central Style of Behavior
4. Similar Experience in Marriage

5. How I Might Act Differently—Currently
6. How I Might Have Acted Differently—In the Past

Now select a pattern of behavior that you would like to change. For example, Self-Assertiveness, Reaction to Criticism, Loneliness, etc. Each of the general areas will become one page of the ledger. Under the column marked "Current Experience," detail several experiences that best describe your behavior in this area. In the next column, "Underlying Feelings," describe them honestly, no matter how unpleasant they may have been. Try to characterize your "Central Style" (Hawk, Dove or Ostrich). Then describe a "Similar Experience in Marriage."

The last two columns are the most important because you will formulate your own suggestions for changing your behavior.

Choose methods of action and change that are feasible for you. For instance, if you have trouble making new friends, it is not necessary to go on a Caribbean cruise. It makes more sense to join a discussion group or a yoga exercise club or an adult-education class. You stack the deck against success if you choose impossible alternatives. Take small, comfortable steps toward change. "Bite off a little less than you can chew" is a good adage in this case.

Growing and changing requires hard work, but the ledger will help to make it easier. When things seem to be going all wrong, look for similar experiences in your ledger and the suggestions you made to yourself about alternate ways of behaving. Suddenly some basic "truths" about your personality or needs will become clear. People do change, and so can you.

But even before change occurs, you will have taken an important and constructive step. You will have gained awareness. Knowing *why* you behave the way you do not only reduces anxiety, it is the beginning of self-knowledge, without which change is impossible.

Seven

Take Action— Exercises

THE next step in your unraveling is to assign yourself specific exercises to modify the behavior that is currently causing you unhappiness. The exercises in this chapter could be the beginning of change and lead to greater insights, stimulating more change. Just as insight stimulates action, action stimulates insight.

For example, a young woman gave herself the exercise of saying no to her fiancé just once, and learned for the first time *why* she had always said yes to him previously, even when she felt furious with herself for doing so. Just as she unconsciously anticipated, he became angry and stormed off, but to her surprise, she was relieved. She realized that she had been afraid not only of his anger, but of facing the truth that she didn't really *like* him. Because she believed she needed him, she had convinced herself that he was what she wanted.

The results of behaving in a certain way may cause you pain, but it is a familiar pain and you are used to it. Feelings of depression and rejection are part of your life, almost like old friends. You know they will pass eventually or you know how to dull the pain. To change your behavior is far more frightening because all change is accompanied by anxiety. Anyone who has suffered anxiety attacks knows how frightening they are. Change means entering new territory, where you may run into new feelings that may hurt more than the old ones and in new places. New behavior means new responses from others, and you may feel safer with the old ones, even if they make you miserable.

You may, for example, consistently agree to do things you don't want to do in order to avoid offending someone or to make that person think you are as nice as you believe you have to be in order to get any kind of acceptance at all. Saying no the first few times will elicit a different response. The other person may react with surprise, raise an eyebrow, but accept your no and say nothing. In that case you're lucky (if you don't rush in to take back your no). Or since you've always said yes, your friend may try to intimidate you back into your familiar behavior. (Most people will not give up slaves or yes men easily. They have, after all, had a free ride—on your shoulders.) Your friend can do this by suggesting that you are selfish or ungrateful, or that you are in a bad mood, or that you don't look well: "Are you sure you're feeling all right?" He (or she) may subtly dangle the carrot of some future reward, or worse, subtly hold out a threat that he'll disappear, drop you, think badly of you if you don't behave like the wonderful person "you used to be."

Be prepared for any one of these reactions, but remember that your aim is to change those behavior patterns that make you unhappy.

———◇———

Dove Action Exercise

If you are a Dove, determine to say no on three different occasions to someone with whom you habitually find yourself in a "servant" role. Write down the other person's reactions each time, and your own feelings about them.

Was your friend shocked? Surprised? Could you read his/her expression? Did it match his/her words? Were you scared? Did your voice tremble? Were you able to make eye contact with the other person as you said no?

How did his/her reaction make you feel each time? Did you experience anxiety later, even if you stayed calm at the time? Were you able to "ride out" your anxiety and try again? Can you remember feeling this same kind of anxiety as a child? As an adolescent? In your previous marriage or close relationship?

Did you ever rebel against being good? It so, what happened? Were you punished? Was love or approval withheld? Did you determine never to rebel again?

Did you feel, in the present instance, that the other person was right, whether he/she expressed it verbally or nonverbally, and that you were perhaps selfish? Did you feel you were right to say no in this case and that the other person was selfish to ask it of you?

Do you think you can say no to this person again? Can you do this in other relationships?

Do you like yourself more?

If the other person's reaction was negative, you undoubtedly experienced tremendous anxiety: "Now he[she] won't like me. I shouldn't have done that. I may never see him[her] again. I must be selfish."

You may experience real pain: "Why do I always feel this way—worried about what someone else thinks of me every minute. Why can't I be happy? Why can't I be liked as other people are, without having to bow and scrape? My friend never does anything for me and yet I hang around. What's the matter with me?"

Don't discount these anxious feelings or believe that you are weak for having them. You are experiencing a "double pain," the pain of the moment and the pain you felt when you were overcome by these feelings in the past, when you were totally dependent on the good will of someone else.

The thought to hang on to is that you are not *helpless* now. You do not *need* anyone's good will at the expense of your own self-respect.

---∾---

Ostrich Action Exercise

If you are an Ostrich, try this with someone you know very well and care about. The next time you are with him (or her), ask a question that you know will get through to him—about his job, his hopes for the future, his fears, his last relationship, his children, the illness or death of someone close to him that you know about (you must be the judge of whether this is appropriate), or a recent disappointment.

Then hear the other person out, even if you feel uncomfortable at first. You don't have to answer, just listen and try to put yourself in his position, feel what he is feeling.

For a minimum of fifteen minutes *don't*, if you become anxious, suggest a movie, or turning on the television, or pick up a paper or magazine.

How did the other person react? What did he say? How did you feel during the exchange? After? Did you find it hard to breathe? Did you feel an impulse to get away, to turn to something else?

Did you feel anxious later, as though you might now become too involved, be taken over by the other's problems? That you are better off staying cool? That this is dangerous and you might get hurt? That you're getting soft and will pay for it?

Whatever your reaction, do you remember feeling this way before? When? What did you do then? How did those around you react? Does it upset you to make any change in yourself or in your way of behaving with others?

Could you repeat this exercise? Do you think you will like yourself more or less with this kind of relating?

---⋄---

Hawk Action Exercise

If you are a Hawk, on a date or the next time you are in a one-to-one situation with someone you know very well, say something good about him/her. By your manner and tone of voice, show that you like him/her, are glad to be with him/her, would like to do something that he/she would enjoy. Ask for suggestions. Check the impulse to say no even if you feel the suggestion is stupid, or not to your taste. Restrain your inclination to correct or criticize the other's ideas, speech, manners, dress. Instead, encourage the other person to talk about himself/herself, and his/her most recent accomplishment. Don't top it with your own, even if you could.

Let go of your nagging voices and consciously tell yourself you are going to have a good time, that you like the person you are with and that it is all right to let up from work.

Thank the other person for his/her company. Don't

make him/her feel guilty that, because of him/her, you stayed up too late, have to work hard tomorrow and shouldn't have gone out at all.

Allow him/her and yourself to experience pleasure.

How did the other person react? Surprised? Bewildered? How did you feel? Were you anxious when you got home? Did you tell yourself you were silly or stupid to try an experiment of this sort? That being nice never got anyone anywhere? That people will begin to take advantage of you? That you must control your feelings? That it is foolish to expect anyone to care how you act? That they have already formed their opinion of you and it's bad, so why bother?

Do you remember behaving this way in your past?

What was the reaction then?

Could you do this exercise again?

Do you like yourself better?

Note: These exercises and the ones that follow for the specific Dove, Ostrich and Hawk types can be expanded and varied endlessly. They are meant to give you some picture of what occurs when you attempt any change, and to warn you that you will experience some anxiety but that it is temporary. Be assured that the pain will lessen with each new attempt and that gradually you will feel better about yourself.

Exercises for Dove Lovers

Objectives:

1. To distinguish between the need to be in love and the genuine feelings of love
2. To control unrealistic fantasies that are based on insecurity rather than on genuine feelings
3. To gain a greater sense of self-worth

I. The next time you believe you are in love, give yourself this test.

   a. List four qualities about him/her you actually *like*.

   b. List four qualities you actively dislike or that you
have questions about when you are being totally
honest.

II. On your next encounter, deliberately withhold flattery or any overt expression of love unless it is totally
spontaneous.

III. Each time you think about the person you are "in
love with," make a mental note of it. What are your
fantasies? Are you slipping into "This will solve all
my problems"? Consciously think about something
else or keep your mind on the task at hand.

IV. Unless there is an emergency, do not telephone or
write the person for five days.

   a. Again, to examine your reactions, do you feel
"dead" or listless or bored when cut off from the
person you love? Ask yourself if this is a familiar
feeling. Did you feel this way in your last close
relationship when your lover was not with you?

V. Plan a night with friends other than your current love.
Dress up just as much as you would if you were
seeing him/her. Determine not to talk about your
romance, good or bad. Make a conscious effort to become involved in what you are doing, focusing on the
event. Were you able to enjoy yourself?

Exercises for Dove Givers

Objectives:

1. To relate to the opposite sex in an environment of
freedom for both, including privacy
2. To reduce instant self-disclosure
3. To learn greater self-appreciation

I. In your next encounter with a member of the opposite sex, concentrate on yourself. Express *your* likes and dislikes. Bite your tongue on all solicitous inquiries and never, *never* offer to sew on a button or run to fetch anything. Allow yourself to be coddled and deferred to—force yourself. Remember, this is an exercise!

II. In *all* encounters for one month, you will control all impulses to "volunteer" your services for anything. If you are asked to volunteer, say that you will let them know tomorrow. Then think very carefully about whether this is something you would really enjoy doing or whether it is something you feel you *must* do. If you feel you must comply, write down all the reasons honestly. You may find you are only trying to gain attention, love or gratitude. If so, say you are unable to help this time. You can do it! It's just for a month.

III. On all dates with new acquaintances during the next three months, however "turned on" you may be, vow to yourself to keep the affair a platonic one for at least two weeks after the first meeting. This is not to prove your virtue, but to teach you to hold back, not to give all of your physical self away immediately as though you had nothing else to offer.

IV. After each encounter, write a detailed account, including the following:

   a. How did I feel about limiting my behavior?

   b. Did I fear I offended my partner by withholding sex?

   c. How was I perceived as a person?

   d. How comfortable was I in an equal role of a receiver as well as a giver?

   e. How would things have been different if I had allowed myself more physical expression?

   f. Compare the way you feel about yourself now with

the way you felt about yourself in previous relationships or in marriage, where you "gave" immediately and continuously.

Exercises for Dove Sufferers

Objectives:

1. To assess realistically your physical complaints and how you use them to relate to and control people
2. To develop the ability to openly express anger and disappointment

  I. Make a list of all current symptoms.
    a. Make an appointment immediately with your doctor or a specialist if necessary to have symptoms investigated.
    b. Follow every recommendation of your doctor.
    c. Vow not to discuss any of your complaints with anyone but your doctor.
  II. Determine that for the next week you will complain one less time, on the average, each day. Decide how many complaints you will allow yourself each day. Keep a careful record, not allowing yourself to exceed your allotted number of complaints.
    a. Each successive week, reduce the daily number of complaints by one.
    b. Make a list of three things you really enjoy doing at least once a week. On any day you exceed the allotted number of complaints, eliminate one enjoyable activity. Each successful week, indulge yourself in one additional experience that you enjoy.
  III. Before leaving your home each day, sit down in a comfortable chair, and starting from your head and moving downward, complain out loud about each and every symptom you feel, or may feel, during the day no matter how small the complaint. Then de-

termine that you will not complain to anyone for the rest of the day.

IV. On a 3" x 5" card write: "I am no more ill than most people around me. There is no need to feel sorry for myself and suffer. I have as much right as others around me to enjoy life." Read this statement prior to leaving the house in the morning. Read it again at 11 A.M., 2 P.M., 5 P.M., 8 P.M., and before sleep.

V. Each evening, make a list of all your grievances during that day, whether against your mate, friends, co-workers or shopkeepers. Determine if they were justifiable. Did you express anger directly? If not, write out a positive, open expression of your anger (e.g., "I feel they let me down and right now I'm very angry about it").

Exercises for Dove and Ostrich Spenders

Objectives:

1. To examine the reasons behind your spending
2. To learn to control the impulse to reward yourself by spending
3. To learn independence and reach real objectives

I. Determine to openly express your feelings of rejection, disappointment or anger in each encounter as it happens.

II. Work out a complete, realistic budget for yourself for one month.

a. List all income. List all regular monthly expenditures: rent, utilities, food. Budget remaining income realistically for clothes, entertainment, cosmetics, sports equipment, and the like. Stick to the budget rigidly for two months.

III. Vow to yourself there will be *no* impulse buying.

a. Each time the "urge" comes over you to buy something unnecessary, force yourself to sit down quietly and examine the reason. Go over the events and encounters of the day, the day before, the day before that, until you find what triggered the "need."

b. Write out the event in detail, whether it was an actual encounter, a painful memory, an imagined slight or an actual rejection. Perhaps your spending pattern will emerge.

IV. Make a list of all the things you would like to do: e.g., play the piano, take a writing course, learn a new language. Be *realistic* in your objectives, but if the activity is something you can afford, do it.

Exercises for Ostrich Lovers

Objectives:

1. To develop awareness of Ostrich qualities in love relationships
2. To develop a capacity for deeper commitments in love relationships

I. Make a list of three recent "love" relationships which lasted six months or longer (of course, if there have been fewer than three, deal with those). For each relationship, write out answers to the following:

a. How much autonomy did you maintain in the relationship, i.e., could you, more or less, do the things you wanted to do?

b. Detail the constraints you felt.

c. Did you find it difficult to verbalize feelings?

d. Did your partner expect you to react emotionally to such a degree that it became uncomfortable for you?

e. At what point did the relationship stop being "fun"?

II. Write out the dictionary definition of "commitment."
   a. Analyze each of your relationships according to the components of this definition.
III. Write out the definition of the word "demand." Write out definition of the word "request." Can you perceive the difference?
   a. Make a list of everything you perceive as a "demand" for two days. Apply dictionary definitions. Were they actually "requests"?
IV. During the next month, make a special point of listening carefully to someone who shares a personal problem with you. If you genuinely feel sympathy, empathy, or wish to help, force yourself to respond with statements that express these sentiments:
   "I'm sorry that . . ."
   "I can understand how you feel . . ."
   "Is there anything I can do to help?"
   a. Are you aware of different reactions from your friend?
   b. Do you feel different? How?

Exercises for Ostrich Teases

Objectives:
1. To gain awareness of your use of teasing as a defense
2. To develop confidence in your ability to communicate without teasing

I. For one day, write down all encounters with members of the opposite sex. Describe in detail your actions. If you teased, describe your feelings immediately prior to the encounter. Were you depressed or feeling negative about yourself? Describe, if possible, what caused these feelings.
   a. Did you feel more positive about yourself after the encounter?
II. List all positive aspects of yourself: physical assets,

personality, talents, etc. Do the same for the negative aspects.

   a. Evaluate the negative aspects. Are they real or imagined? How do you usually handle them in daily encounters? Could you, with very little effort, improve these negative aspects? Write a description of how.

III. Determine that for the next two weeks, in any conversation with a member of the opposite sex, you will not include sexual overtones. If they are initiated by the other person, you will not respond.

IV. After each encounter, write out a detailed account of your feelings and the reactions of others to you.

   a. Can you rely on qualities other than your sex appeal to feel like an attractive, desirable person?

   b. Did you find that you could communicate with members of the opposite sex without teasing or flirtation as a defense?

 V. Develop new skills to gain greater confidence in social situations.

VI. Broaden your interests outside yourself. Read one national news magazine each week, as well as a daily paper.

   a. Offer your time to help a friend or neighbor with chores or errands.

Exercises for Ostrich Show-Offs

Objectives:

1. To develop confidence in your ability to communicate without showing off

2. To become aware of your use of showing off as a defense against closeness

IMPORTANT: If showing off occurs solely after the consumption of alcohol, seek professional help or help through volunteer agencies (like Alcoholics Anonymous). Showing off may disappear if there is better control of alcoholic consumption.

I. Think of the person you admire most for his/her ease of manner and quiet friendliness in social situations. Remember the last time you saw that person in a social situation. How did you behave at that same affair? Were you showing off?
   a. What do you think was the reaction of others to your "performance"?
   b. Now imagine yourself in the same situation behaving as much as possible like the person you admire.
   c. Can you describe what might be the reactions of others to the different you?
   d. Review these steps for fifteen minutes before your next social engagement.
II. On a 3″ x 5″ card write: "There is no need to be on stage. My friends should and will appreciate me more if I don't behave flamboyantly. I really don't have to act that way to be liked." Carry the card with you at all times. Read it before leaving in the morning, prior to lunch, at 6 P.M., or before going out for the evening.
III. If you are at a social event and you realize you have been "doing your act" again, *you must leave immediately.*
IV. Keep a detailed "social" diary. After each event, write a detailed description of your behavior.
   a. Were you showing off?
   b. Honestly analyze the reactions of those with you to your behavior.
   c. Do you feel your behavior was important to the success of the event?
   d. What would have been the results of the event if you had behaved differently?

Exercises for Ostrich Addicts

Objectives:
1. To clarify your addiction
2. To take some positive steps in reducing your "addiction"
3. To develop helpful attitudes if further professional help is sought

IMPORTANT: Ostrich Addicts usually need outside help. Certified and licensed professionals are often required, or self-help organizations such as Alcoholics or Gamblers Anonymous.

I. Keep careful records (this is important!).
    a. Precisely define your addiction: gambling, overworking, drinking, etc.
    b. Keep a *daily* log.
       1. Enter your thoughts every time you think of your addiction.
       2. Enter your actions whenever you take a drink, make a bet, smoke a joint, etc.
       3. Make tally marks to keep an accurate count of thoughts and action. Keep a record of how many seconds or minutes you thought or acted on your addiction each time you did.
       4. Make relevant comments to amplify and clarify the quality of thoughts or actions after each day.
    c. Note daily, weekly and monthly trends. Note if you have typical, predictable patterns in your addiction.
II. Break through your justification process. Most addicts are great rationalizers who excuse their behavior and find innumerable reasons for not changing at any particular time. Determine to change some portion of your addicted behavior.
    a. Select one thought and one behavior you wish to change.

    b. Determine to reduce the thought and behavior by one time each the following day.

    c. Maintain that reduction for three days.

    d. Reduce by one more unit, etc.

Prior to performing step II, decide on the number of attempts you will make before you consider the effort unsuccessful. There should be a minimum and an absolute maximum of three attempts. If it doesn't work, resolve—without *any* qualification whatsoever—to make an appointment with a qualified professional. There are social agencies with quite reasonable fees or no fees at all, so lack of income should be no excuse.

Exercises for Ostrich Tune-Outs

Objectives:

1. To become comfortable with expressing emotions, both verbally and nonverbally

2. To enter some relationships on more than a superficial basis

  I. Make a list of as many "feeling" words as you can.

    a. Increase your list by looking up synonyms and antonyms in a dictionary or thesaurus.

    b. Use each of the words in writing a complete sentence starting with the word "I," e.g., "I hurt easily."

    c. Repeat the above, but this time write out an action statement between you and another person, e.g., "I am so angry with you I could hit you."

 II. Write three scripts, in dialogue, between you and another person, using themes of love, anger, fear.

Example:

JOAN: Are you ever frightened of anything?

ME: Well, not really.

JOAN: You don't sound so sure about it.

ME: I guess I've been scared at times.

JOAN: Of what?

ME: Of talking to people . . . about anything serious.

III. Choose a person you genuinely care for (parent, friend, relative, mate).

    a. Decide that during the next week you will express your tender, affectionate feelings toward that person.

    b. Each time, write out what you said and the response you received. How did you feel about saying those things? About how it was received?

    c. After two weeks, increase the number of affectionate statements by one until at least one genuine feeling statement can be made daily to that person.

    d. If possible, add another person you care for and go through a similar process, so that there are now two people toward whom you are able to communicate genuine feelings.

    e. Be sensitive to nonverbal expressions as well as verbal ones.

    Checkpoints:

      1. Did you make eye contact during your statement?

      2. Did you find it difficult in the beginning?

      3. Were you able to touch the other person?

      4. Did you listen to the response?

      5. Did you move away quickly after the statement or turn your body in such a way as to avoid further communication?

Exercises for Ostrich Runners

Objectives:

1. To structure a balanced day

2. To accept yourself without anxiety

I. Make four columns. In Column I, list all those activities during the week that are essential. In Column II, list activities that are important but, on occasion, could be avoided. In Column III, list activities that are not essential, but that you really look forward to doing. In Column IV, list those activities which are not important and, in fact, not overly exciting—those activities you use for "fillers."

   a. Review the categories very carefully so that each activity ends up in the correct column. Take the *easiest* activity to give up in Column IV and do give it up the following day.

   b. Taking one activity at a time, and giving yourself a week between eliminating activities, allow Column IV activities to disappear from your schedule.

   c. After two weeks without activities in Column IV, start the same process with Column III.

   d. Review activities in Columns I and II. Make sure they are really important. Restructure your week so that there is ample "breathing space" throughout the day.

II. During the leisure time you have now acquired, say the following twice every day, before 11 A.M. and once between 2 and 4 P.M.:

"I [John Jones] have the right to relax and enjoy myself. There is no real value in being frenzied and harried. I am not perfect, but no one else is either. Therefore I will accept those things I can't change in myself, and slowly change those things I can and want to change in myself."

Exercises for Hawk Lovers

Objectives:
1. To acknowledge your Hawk qualities, however unpleasant
2. To experience non-Hawk relationships

I. Write a paragraph description of your last close relationship. What form of control did you use to get your way: Manipulation? Force? Smothering? Withdrawal?

II. In your next close relationship, determine you will not utilize any manipulation in mutual decision making.

III. At work, or in a social situation involving others, make a genuine effort to:

   a. Listen carefully.

   b. Hold back any negative comments about another opinion for at least one hour.

   c. Encourage others to comment fully on your views, even if they are opposed to them.

   d. Analyze your behavior, including your use of flattery, to uncover your methods of control. Do this in writing.

   e. Respect the suggestions of others even if they don't *seem* to have as much merit as your ideas.

IV. Do the above for one month, recording your reactions in a notebook before going to sleep, checking your progress as you go along.

Exercises for Hawk Heros/Heroines

Objectives:

1. To recognize that you can participate without feeling you *must* win

2. To expand your ability to relax and enjoy life

I. In the next competitive sport or game, like tennis, golf, cards or word games:

   a. Record your feelings as the game began.

      1. Were you tense, excited, elated?

   b. What were your reactions if you made a bad move?

   c. How did you feel if you won? Did you gloat?

    d. How did you feel if you lost? Did you sulk?

    e. Did you congratulate the winner? Commiserate with the loser?

    f. Did winning make you anxious?

II. Make no effort to win in your next non-job competitive encounter. Try simply to enjoy yourself.

    a. How did you feel?

III. The next time you begin to compare yourself to anyone else, favorably or unfavorably, stop and think about what you are doing, and why.

IV. Deliberately stop yourself when you feel the urge to triumph over someone verbally. Write your reactions.

Exercises for Hawk Perfectionists

Objectives:

1. To learn to curb your compulsion
2. To learn to take reasonable criticism without becoming angry at yourself or the other person

  I. Vow that for one twenty-four-hour period you will not, beyond ordinary neatness like hanging up your clothes, straighten or tidy up *anything*.

 II. During that same twenty-four-hour period you will also *not* correct anyone about their mistakes or imperfections.

III. On a pad that you will keep with you, note down each time you feel the impulse to correct or straighten up.

    a. Also note each time you are unable to control the impulse, and the reaction of the other person involved.

IV. Keep trying until you have successfully completed one twenty-four-hour period without giving in to your compulsion. Then try for a forty-eight-hour period.

 V. When you are criticized, write out the encounter.

    a. Was your anger unreasonable? Did you defend yourself beyond what was necessary?

    b. Could you have reacted in a more reasonable way? How?

    c. If there was a mistake on your part, was the criticism justified? Was the mistake so terrible? Could you make yourself simply say, "You're right, and not blame anyone?

Exercises for Hawk Blamers

Objectives:

1. To see the positives in life without blaming others for things that don't turn out as planned
2. To minimize guilt about having a nice comfortable day, with successes, productivity and simple contentment

  I. Upon awakening each morning, before breakfast, vow the following:

"I [Jane/John Smith] will see the positive side in everything that happens today. I'll blame no one. I'll look for reasonable explanations when things go wrong, and not assign 'villains.' "

  II. Each night, write a detailed schedule for the next day.

    a. Next to each activity, describe two ways in which the activity may not turn out according to plan.

    b. Next, give one opinion, a reasonable one, for why it could fail.

    c. Develop an attitude, in writing, about why, even if it fails, it will really not be so bad.

Exercises for Hawk Manipulators

Objectives:

1. To learn to recognize those times when you are manipulating, and to discover why
2. To develop trust in other people's ability and to trust yourself to others

I. Make a list of people with whom you related the previous day (spouse, fellow employees, boss, friend).
   a. Next to each name, write out how you "pushed," "needled" or "manipulated."
   Patterns to look for:
      1. Is it one particular person or group? Define your relationship. Is the other person in a position of authority? Is your manifestation passive? Is it competitive?
      2. Does it occur at a particular time of day? When your tolerance for frustration is low? When you're tired? When you feel threatened?
   b. In a new column or paragraph, reconstruct each situation where you instigated or manipulated, and write a nonmanipulative alternative.
   c. Do this daily for a month.
II. Determine the person whom you manipulate the most, and the most easily.
   a. What are you doing to manipulate that person?
   b. Write an account of each incident, including what you felt, and how you think the other person felt.
   c. The next time you are with this person, use every effort not to manipulate at all. Bend over backwards to control the urge, and be extra understanding and benevolent. Be aware of your tendency to *want* to manipulate.

Manipulation (aggressiveness) is not assertiveness: Assertiveness is forthrightly expressing your genuine feelings without showing disrespect or belittling anyone.

Exercises for Hawk Intellectuals

Objectives:
1. To inhibit the use of language and thought as a weapon
2. To learn to accept the stimulation others can give you

I. Decide that for the next week you will:
   a. Use less pretentious language
   b. Listen to the ideas of others without responding immediately
   c. Employ "feeling," tender adjectives and expressions when speaking with a friend or family member
      Examples:
      "I enjoyed being with you today."
      "I like your suggestion very much."
      "I'm sorry I can't come tomorrow. I would have enjoyed spending the day with you."

II. Decide not to "needle," belittle or embarrass anyone for the next week. After each hour, in a notebook that you will carry with you, write down all those instances when you lost control and needled or embarrassed someone.
   a. Each day, write down such statements (you may paraphrase) as you made them during the day.
   b. Rewrite the statements so that they show some feeling and softness.
      Example:
      "If you think that is the answer, you obviously haven't really grasped the problem. I really think you should get the facts straight before offering an opinion."
      Change to:
      "Well, you may be right. I hadn't thought of it in quite that way. Thanks for pointing it out to me."

III. Choose someone you like very much. When you are with that person during the next week, attempt to communicate by touching rather than talking during some part of each meeting. For example, instead of verbalizing appreciation for something done, take the person's hand and give it a warm squeeze. Or instead of saying goodbye, blow a kiss, or kiss the person.

Part Three

Make New Patterns

Eight

Finding a
New Partner

THE best way to find a marriage partner is *not* to look
for one. Concentrate instead on having a wonderful time—
meeting new people, learning new things, seeing new
places, conquering new fields. Then if you happen to meet
someone you'd consider marrying along the way, it will
be frosting on the cake of a fulfilling life.

Approaching your new life in this manner will eliminate
the all-too-apparent desperation that sets in when people
set out deliberately to find a new mate.

Open Up

You've been told, or you have read, that you should
join groups, take classes, volunteer or develop your special
talents so often that I hesitate to say it again. But it cannot
be stressed enough.

You will never find out how much you can grow unless
you take that first big step and open up your mind to new
experiences, and no one else will know how much you
have to offer if you confine yourself to your job, your

apartment and the same circle of friends you've been with for years.

Each new action leads to another act.

Each new thing you learn leads to something new to learn.

Each new person you meet leads to another person.

Jean, forty, and depressed after her divorce, took a typing course simply to force herself out of the house. In the class she met a young Greek exchange student who was terribly homesick and began telling her stories of Greece. He made his country come so vividly to life for her that she began reading everything she could find about it, even learning the language. She has gone to Greece for her vacation every year since, and has made a whole new circle of friends through relatives of the student.

The Greek student she befriended was years younger than Jean, so had she only been looking for a husband, she might never have opened up to him. She would thus have lost the opportunity to add a great deal of richness and beauty to her life. She communicated her new excitement and enthusiasm to a man in her office who had never noticed her before and they are now talking about seeing Greece together next year.

Hank had a similar experience. As a newly divorced man he was a godsend to hostesses looking for a single man to make the table even at the last moment. He had avoided these invitations for months, but one night his loneliness drove him to accept. His "partner" at dinner was an aging operatic soprano. Hank had always loathed opera, but he enjoyed talking to this still-vital and sparkling old lady. When he invited her to dinner at his apartment, she brought an album of *Tosca* which, in spite of his misgivings, she insisted on playing. During dinner she told him the story of the opera, acting out some of the parts as she went along, and completely captivating his imagination. "For the first time I opened my mind to the music,

and when she played the album I *heard* it. She had made
it come alive for me."

He became an opera buff, attending performances whenever possible and starting a record collection. Because he
was not bent on finding a new marriage partner, his mind
was open to other experiences. Indirectly, this experience
did lead to marriage for Hank. While in a record store to
purchase a new recording of *Norma*, he got into a discussion with a young woman about various sopranos and
their roles—and you know the rest.

We all have capacities to grow that we don't know exist.
There are virtually dozens of extracurricular avenues open
to you: local political groups, volunteer hospital work,
local theater groups (start one if that's your interest), con-
servation groups, Parents Without Partners, classes in typing, languages, yoga, belly dancing, karate.

Having been hurt, you are naturally resistant to expos-
ing yourself to new people and new experiences, but that
is precisely what is required.

Take the First Step

Here is an exercise to help break down that resistance
and the normal inertia that sets in when anyone suggests
action.

When you finish reading this section, stop, and decide
to follow up on something you have always wanted to do
or learn. Look at once in the Yellow Pages for listings, or
in your daily newspaper for some schools, or call a friend
who always seems to know about these things (most people
have a friend like that). Write down the names and telephone numbers, and if possible, call immediately. If it's
impossible at the moment (too late at night, for instance),
put the number on your bathroom mirror so that it will
be the first thing you see in the morning, and call then.
Remember, it's making that first move that is the most
difficult. Don't allow yourself any excuses for procrastina-

tion. If the enrollment is closed, register for the next term, or look up private teachers. Call that friend again, or put up a notice about your intentions on the bulletin board at your office. Make a pledge to yourself that you will be involved in something before the week is out.

You may not meet the person you are going to marry at a drama class or as a nurse's aide, but you will be getting out of the house and into action. You will be *visible* to an entirely new set of people and, new mate or not, your life will be better.

Going to a class or a meeting means you must get dressed. That in itself can change your mood, make you feel part of the mainstream of life again. Never underestimate the power of getting dressed up—or if you're a woman, getting made up!

Kate, a woman with a fine sense of the ridiculous, told me this story about herself: "I had been depressed for days. Really depressed. I had never experienced anything like it. It was the middle of winter and I just stood all day looking out my window at the bleak cold skyline. I thought it looked just the way I felt inside my head—gray and dull and hopeless.

"I had blown my chances for a job I wanted, and I'd just made a couple of really stupid decisions. My marriage had ended. I was over forty and looked it. There were sleeping pills in my medicine cabinet and I started wondering if there were enough to do the job. I had never thought about suicide before, but I was so sick of my life and so incredibly tired. I thought it would be such a relief to take the pills and just lie down and sleep. I went into the bathroom to get the pills and got a look at myself in the bathroom mirror. My hair was in strings, my face a sort of pale gray and I was in a disgusting old kimono. I thought about my friend across the street. She'd be the first one to find me, then her husband, then the police and the neighbors. I couldn't let anyone see me like this—even dead.

"So I showered and washed my hair, brushed it dry and put on my best green velour lounging robe. The green made me look even paler, so I decided to put on some make-up. I did a full job—foundation, mascara, lipstick and plenty of blusher.

"I reached for my pills, but then I got a really good look at myself. I looked pretty sensational—hair all fluffy, face gleaming and glowing with Revlon's best and the green velour was smashing. What a shame, I thought, that I wouldn't be around to hear my friend's reaction. I really looked too good to waste.

"Then it hit me—here I was convinced I was suicidal and worrying about my looks. I started to laugh. And it completely broke the spell I was in. I realized I didn't want to die—I didn't even want to sleep. I wanted to live as much and as long as it was possible."

Get Involved

Throwing yourself fully into whatever you choose to do is the best way to lose your self-consciousness. The more involved you are, the less needy you'll feel. Your attitude about yourself will become more positive, and so will the attitude of others toward you.

Do you recall ever admiring a person who always stays safely on the sidelines, who never offers to help when there's work to be done, who never speaks up in discussions for fear he may be wrong or ridiculed? Of course not—and neither does anyone else. Go all the way with enthusiasm. It will give you a new vitality—the kind that makes people want to know you.

Involvement doesn't mean you have to be the leader. It means making suggestions, speaking out on issues, listening. It means realizing you have the capacity to relate to others and to act on your own, not as an appendage of another person. This knowledge will make you a better partner if you marry again.

Creative Solitude

It is an interesting phenomenon that as you open up and become involved in living and learning, spending weekends alone, for example, will not loom so threateningly. In fact, you will find that you take new pleasure in your own company. The man I wrote of earlier, who came to love opera, began to look forward to Saturdays as a day when performances were broadcast on the radio and he could quietly enjoy them by himself.

Anyone who has been married can tell you that marriage is not a cure-all for loneliness. After the honeymoon you will still find yourself away from your partner a good part of the day. Marriage is not a metamorphosis. You will still be you. Any attempt to live your life through your partner will ultimately be suffocating, even if it seems viable during the first "two-hearts-beating-as-one" stage. Guilt and contempt for your "immersed self" will eventually erupt.

On the most pragmatic level, there is the inescapable fact that we are all prone to chance, and we all face death. Your partner may die. If you are not a functioning, fully developed person when this happens, someone who is not afraid of periods of solitude, you may find it far more difficult to pick up the pieces of your lost self and make it on your own.

Learn to schedule time for yourself, periods of "digesting" your experiences and feelings. While you should seek involvement and activity, you should not shut out the quiet periods by yourself, which are part of real self-fulfillment.

Growing Up

In America, maturity has connotations of stodginess and dullness, rather than what it really is—growing up. Maturity means knowing that life is not a continual "rose garden," that even with the best of intentions, you don't always succeed, that what works for one person may be disastrous for you. It also means giving up some of the illusions that have crippled rather than helped you; for instance, the belief that there is only one person in the world—just for you. The truth is that if you were to change your location from, say, Chicago to Los Angeles, there would be a different "one." Other illusions that must be dispensed with are:

Romantic love is the only kind to strive for.
Having someone to love you is a ticket to a life of bliss.
You are not whole unless you are part of a couple.
Marriage is a haven where you will be safe from life's hard knocks because you will be taken care of.

These are only a few of the illusions we have been "programmed" to expect from marriage. Grownups know that romantic love is short-lived and that something deeper must replace it if the marriage is to last; they know that marriage is not a place where you let down and "take for granted," but that it demands more hard work and understanding than you may ever have faced before.

Opening up, getting involved and growing up—all are necessary steps to take. In finding a partner by not looking for one, you may meet the most interesting person you have ever known—yourself.

———◇———

The Not-Looking Approach for Finding a Partner

Dos and Don'ts for Doves

If you join a group, don't go overboard in your efforts to get instant approval. You don't always have to be the one who empties the garbage, starts the fire and brings four covered dishes when everyone else brings two. Nor should you be the group chauffeur. Become involved and do your share—maybe even a little more— but don't allow yourself to be or feel used. Approve of yourself and you will stop feeling on trial.

THE KEY WORD IS "RESTRAINT"

You may have to *practice* restraint. Try to hold something in reserve. This doesn't mean being closed. But when you confide too much too soon, aren't you turning your life over to someone else? Aren't you hoping he/she will take over the responsibility, share your guilt, relieve you of anxiety?

If you give your all at first meeting, you're saying that your life isn't worth very much so you give it away. The person to whom you are confiding cannot help but wonder if what he says to you will be broadcast to the next person you meet.

DON'T abuse the shoulder you lean on.

DON'T be afraid to have and express your views. Echoes are boring.

DON'T use sex to ingratiate yourself.

DON'T exaggerate your love. Allow it to grow naturally. You existed before you fell in love. Love that endures doesn't need added drama.

DON'T use minor ailments to get out of things you don't want to cope with.

Do learn to live with anxiety. Know that everyone has moments of unreasoning fear. If you go through anxiety attacks alone occasionally, you will see that they will not destroy you, and you will emerge stronger.

Do remember that you are no longer helpless. You can be your own mother and father now and you can decide to be a good parent to yourself.

Do recognize that you can't "lose" yourself permanently or live through someone else.

Dos and Don'ts for Ostriches

Cut down on running and joining, and become really involved in one or two projects that truly interest you or where you can make a contribution. And remember that once there, just answering the roll call doesn't end your obligation, although your natural ability to pull back and observe will stand you in good stead. You undoubtedly know more than you have ever put to the test. Plunge in and follow through.

THE KEY WORD IS "RISK"

No one can run forever, and although you may escape some pain, you will also avoid much of what makes life meaningful. A life without passion is not worth living. If you are never there to suffer disappointment, you are also absent for the deeper joys and fulfillments. To break your pattern you will have to break out of your detachment, break down your defenses, break through your fears.

Don't withdraw from a friend who you feel is beginning to cling. Recognize that it is your friend's anxiety about your detachment that makes him/her cling. This may give you the compassion to deal with it in a kinder way.

Don't be afraid to talk about your need to remain detached. It may enable another person to recognize that your moving away doesn't constitute a rejection of him/her. It is *your* need. This won't come easily to you, but try it.

Do make an effort to imagine how your withdrawals affect a person who is fond of you.

Do spend some time with a prospective partner that is not structured—where there is no television, for example. If this produces panic, you are not ready to marry again.

Do widen your horizons, set your goals higher. You have nothing to lose but your boredom.

Do proceed slowly so that you don't scare yourself away. The person you hide from most successfully is yourself, so you will have to get acquainted slowly. As you do, you will be able to get closer to others.

Dos and Don'ts for Hawks

Just as an experiment, try *not* to take over. It could be a first step in breaking a pattern, and it might be relaxing to sit back, at least temporarily, and let someone else have center stage. Observe the group's reaction and your own when you do. Give your support to someone else in the group. Encourage someone to speak who never does. You'll probably wind up running things again, but you may learn something during your vacation from power.

THE KEY WORD IS "RELEASE"

Release your need to control and you may release your ability to love and to enjoy life. Learn to have compassion for yourself and you will find that you have more for others. Remember, people do not judge you as harshly as you judge yourself. Too often you are projecting your own merciless standards onto others' expectations of you, so it's no wonder you go armed and expect the worst. *You* are your severest critic. Let up—you won't fall apart (your secret fear) and you don't need to whip yourself into shape every day. You are not so much unloving as afraid you are unlovable. That you are harder on yourself than you are on others is small comfort to those you hurt.

> DON'T waste your energies getting even with or showing your ex how much better you're doing without him/her.
> DON'T control by giving gifts or playing the benefactor.
> DON'T be manipulative. You may get your way temporarily, but you will never be sure of what you have really gained.
>
> Do let go of your last marriage and don't compare every new person favorably or otherwise with your ex or with former loves. Learn from the past; don't dwell on it.

Do think about what it would be like to have an equal partner, one you could respect, who wouldn't be intimidated.

Do give yourself credit for your good points.

Nine

What Makes a Good Marriage?

No matter what the mix or match, a good marriage requires certain elements to make it work. From my observation of both good and bad marriages throughout the years, the elements that follow seem to be universal and ought to be carefully considered before you marry again.

Since we all have Dove, Ostrich and Hawk tendencies to a greater or lesser degree, you may find it helpful to look at all categories under each component of a good marriage.

Being There

It may seem simplistic to say you have to be physically present in order to make a marriage work, but not being there is an established factor in the breakup of many marriages. "She was never there when I got home" or

"He is never home" are often the first lines I hear when a husband or wife comes in for marriage counseling.

The dialogue in these marriages apparently goes something like this:

> HARRIET: Well, look who's here. I'd almost forgotten what you looked like.
>
> ROGER: Come on, Harriet, you know there are good reasons why I haven't been home this week. Monday I had to work late. Tuesday, same thing. Wednesday is poker night, and—
>
> HARRIET: And Thursday you had to drive your mother somewhere. I suppose I should be grateful it's Friday and say thank you for dropping in.

While it's true that our way of life provides many "good reasons" to be away from home—business trips, professional meetings, bridge nights, PTA meetings, church groups and the like—if a marriage is to work, it is important to establish that time together is of first priority. Otherwise, marriage partners are no more than casual roommates, and home no more than a way station used to refuel and change before going on to the next activity. There is no "right" amount of time, but if you are separated far more than you are together outside of working hours, there will eventually be trouble. A successful marriage takes two people.

Doves

This isn't usually a problem for you. On the contrary, you might have to worry about being there too much, being too available, waiting too passively for your partner to come home—to entertain you, provide you with stimulation or simply to take you out of yourself. Your being fully alive will make being there a pleasure, not an obligation for you and for your partner.

Ostriches

Since distancing is part of your life style, this requirement may take some soul-searching on your part. Consider honestly if marriage is for you. On the other hand, isn't it time you stop running and face your demons? You may find they have lost their power through the years, and that being close does not necessarily mean being devoured. If you face yourself, you may enjoy facing your partner.

Hawks

Your work and getting ahead is usually your excuse for being absent. Ask yourself what you are working and getting ahead *for*. If your goal includes a good marriage, you have to be a participant. Conversely, you may feel your presence is essential to keep everything at home going *your* way. Consider being there without being in command. Your partner might enjoy being there with you more often.

—◇—

Talking

Next to "He [or she] is never home," the second biggest complaint I hear is "He [or she] never talks to me" or "We don't talk about anything important." A research study I read recently concluded that the average amount of time a husband and wife actually spent talking during an average day was—ten minutes. A few monosyllables during the breakfast rush, a bit more before and during dinner, the comments between television programs and the newspaper, and making the decision to go to bed constitute "communication" for many couples. Interestingly, the research found that the amount of conversation increased as couples approached divorce. Then, suddenly, they had a great deal to talk about.

Talking does not mean merely exchanging information about the weather, the children and the day's mishaps; it means letting your partner know where you are, emotionally, physically and intellectually. That this is rare is demonstrated time and time again when couples come to me for counseling and begin to air their grievances. The astonishment that greets these disclosures is a sure indication of how little the couple communicated, so much so that I often stop to ask, "Did you two ever really *talk* to each other?"

Doves

You tend to talk too much—or too little. Too much talk about trivia is sometimes your way of hiding your nervousness about whether or not you are loved or accepted. What happened at the office or at the grocer's might even be amusing in small doses, but there's a big world out there to learn about.

And there are your own *real* feelings to express. Don't expect your partner to guess what you want, or to figure out why you are sulking. Speak up.

Ostriches

You use conversation as a shield rather than a bridge, or you remain silent—which says more than you think it does. If you felt your last partner drove you to the newspaper or TV set or out the door because they never said anything "interesting," recognize your contribution to this state of affairs. It takes two to make good conversation, and your partner may not have talked so much or so frantically if he/she had received any real response from you. Try not to bury your grievances. Face your feelings— positive and negative—and express them to your mate. Otherwise your relationship will die for lack of nourishment.

Hawks

Try talking *to*, not *at*, your next partner. Talking isn't a string of commands, a lecture or a sermon. It is give-and-take.

If you use words as a club, don't be surprised if the person you are clubbing goes underground and uses guerrilla tactics against you or simply deserts the arena. This may be the only way he/she can get through to you.

If you retaliate with the silent treatment, you may win the battle but wind up talking to yourself.

---⌒---

Listening

Really listening is a creative act. It means reading the unspoken language of the eyes, the stance of the body, the slumped shoulder and the expression that belies the words. It means hearing "I'm low right now and need some stroking" behind the hearty "I'm fine." It means sensing the hurt or pride of accomplishment behind the casual recounting of some event. For instance:

> TOM: And then I told him . . . hey, are you listening or reading the paper?
> MEG: *(Looking up from the paper guiltily)* Don't be silly. I heard every word. You told your boss you didn't pad your expense account and then what happened?
> TOM: Forget it. The paper is obviously more interesting to you. Go back to it.

Tom was right. Meg was not really hearing what he had to say. He wanted to do more than tell her a story. He was looking for some assurance that what he had done was all right—that someone was on his side.

Doves

Sometimes people simply want you to listen—not to solve their problems. You can't fix everything, so don't try. Don't exhaust yourself by being *too* available to hear others' woes. Your time is valuable to you. And to listen does not mean you have to agree with the speaker.

Ostriches

You are the master at selective hearing, registering only what is pleasant and doesn't require a solution or action on your part. Tune in all the way. Ignoring a problem won't make it disappear. What you don't know *can* sometimes hurt you.

Hawks

Listen! Don't finish other people's sentences. You don't always know what they are going to say even if you are sure you do. And don't frame your answer in advance. Hear the other person out first. The next words you hear may *not* be an attack, or merely "filler" until it's your turn to speak again.

———◇———
Touching

It is always astonishing to me how many couples find it difficult to express affection by touching. Nothing erotic, just plain touching: sitting close enough to feel the other's body; taking his (or her) hand; hold him/her close for a moment during times of stress to let him/her know you are there; sleeping with one arm over his/her hip.

For many couples, the only physical contact that takes place is during sex. It is small wonder that so many people, men as well as women, feel "used." From my observation, the less physical contact there is in nonsexual moments, the less tenderness is expressed in sex.

One woman put it this way: "People talk about foreplay as if it is the five minutes before intercourse. Actually, foreplay is everything that happens during the day, before you go to bed with your husband."

Doves

A little touching goes a long way. It is in your nature to want some physical evidence of love. Be careful that touching doesn't become smothering, and don't ask too much in return. No one likes to kiss or cuddle on demand, or to be constantly fussed over.

Ostriches

Try it. You may have hated to be touched when you were growing up because it was excessive or forced upon you. If *you* take the initiative, you won't feel you are complying. The right touch at the right time is worth a million words.

Hawks

It is not unmanly to hold hands, and you won't be betraying the sisterhood if you caress him instead of correcting him. Often it takes more strength to hold out a hand in love than it does to hold up a fist in anger.

----◇----

Empathizing

Putting yourself in your partner's head and heart takes some mental energy and a leap of the imagination, but is one of the true rewards of a marriage to know that someone really does "know" how you feel.

You may recognize that your partner is overreacting to

a situation, to a disappointment or to a rejection, and be tempted to say, "But that's ridiculous, stop being childish." Empathy would require that for a few moments you project yourself into his/her feelings, and experience the event as he/she must be experiencing it. Only then will you be able to comment, advise or sympathize in a manner that will be helpful and comforting to your partner.

Doves

Staying in your own skin is often so difficult for you that empathizing may take on shades of self-annihilation. You may feel this is your forte, but is it? Do you get into another's head to understand him/her, or because you are not comfortable in your own?

Being able to feel "with" another person when he/she is down means just that. It does *not* mean going down to the depths with him/her—and staying there.

Ostriches

Paradoxically, you are often good at sensing the inner feelings and even despair of other people. And you can, because of your detached attitude, offer cool and reasoned advice—as long as you're not called upon to become involved yourself. Take the next step. It's not possible to remain by a bystander in a good marriage.

Hawks

You pick up distress signals easily enough, but you either read them wrong or come on with such a heavy hand that your partner soon learns to monitor what he/she sends out. Belittling or putting down someone's fears is not empathizing.

Think before you speak. Be sure the advice you give is for someone else's own good, not for your own. Empathy means understanding how the other person feels, not how you think he *should* be feeling. And remember, you can't grasp other people's feelings when you are busy riding rough-shod over your own. With you, empathy should begin at home.

———◇———

Enrichment

Each partner in a marriage enriches the other by bringing his/her unique personality, gifts, imagination, special skills—and friends—to the marriage.

"My wife taught me how to raise plants. She's the expert"; "My husband introduced me to the ballet. I used to hate it"; "We love traveling together. One of us drives and the other map-reads and we both laugh a lot"; "We're celebrating my wife's promotion. I'm proud of her." These statements come from happy couples who have learned the art of enrichment. They are not threatened by each other's differences or development. They relish them.

Enrichment can mean everything from finding a new vacation spot you can share together to developing a long-buried talent and bringing the resultant glow to the marriage. A happy, fulfilled and secure person obviously gives a lot more to a marriage than one who is unhappy, frustrated and insecure. Just as sharing new experiences enriches a marriage with happy memories, so do two people, each growing to their fullest extent, enrich the marriage with renewed vitality and enthusiasm.

Doves

You may be happy to bask in your partner's growth but be terrified of your own. You associate ambition and assertiveness with hostility. They are not the same. Expand your horizons and you will expand those of your partner. It's better to give up a relationship than to give up yourself.

Ostriches

Dreaming up a new way to cook lobsters, to arrange the living room or to make love may come easily to you. So may enriching materially. It's the in-depth giving you may balk at. Think about the best moments in your life with another person. This will give you a clue to the real nature of enrichment in a marriage.

Hawks

You can be counted upon to come up with new plans and projects to keep a marriage from getting dull. Trouble begins if they aren't carried out your way. Then you become openly angry or subtly disrupt things by giving contrary directions or leaving out essential ingredients. You don't always have to do the enriching. Allow your partner to be your partner. Sometimes, two heads *are* better than one.

———◇———

Sexual Compatibility

Sex in a marriage may be regarded as a microcosm of the relationship in its entirety. It is rare that a marriage has everything going for it except sex, and even rarer that a marriage has good sex and little else.

We are too much at the mercy of our emotions to separate sex from the rest of us. If we are angry or feel temporarily defeated, if we are worried or jealous or even guilty, it will show up in our sexual responses. It is true some people are able to compartmentalize better than others, but usually not for long. Ultimately the sexual relationship is affected along with other areas, or becomes so impersonal that it can hardly be said to be successful.

The most common complaints about sexual dysfunctioning are ones that cannot be cured by a sex manual alone. A man who turns away from his wife immediately after the sex act may be expressing more than a lack of knowledge about his wife's needs. He may be expressing more hostility than is readily apparent, just as a woman's frigidity may be only a part of her holding back every kind of giving, emotionally as well as physically.

Doves

Pleasing is part of your nature, but you too deserve to be pleased. Sex should be a mutual decision and a mutual pleasure. Faking orgasm generally goes with faking in other areas of the relationship. And repressed anger can show up in repressed sexual response. Better to put the anger in the situation it belongs than to use sex as the arena. Masochism and martyrdom have never made a good sexual relationship or a good marriage, only a sick one.

Ostriches

Variety in your technique can be more rewarding than a variety of partners. Remember also that technique is no substitute for tenderness. Sex may be the one area where you get at least physically close, but for real closeness, you have to risk more. Spend some time, before and after sex, talking and holding. See if you can stay in bed for thirty minutes after sex without going to sleep, to the refrigerator, or worst of all, out the door. Tell your mate how you felt about the experience and encourage his/her confidences. You may learn that there's more to sex than sex.

Hawks

The marriage bed is not another battleground and there should be one place that you don't compete. Relax and let your partner relax. Neither of you has to be perfect to enjoy sex. Make a conscious effort to turn off your critical switch. And allow your partner to initiate some sexual advances occasionally. No one wants to play "follow the leader" all of the time.

———◇———

Commitment

The requirement that supersedes all others in a good marriage is commitment. Since this is a concept that seemingly has gone out of style, it is no wonder that our divorce rate continues to climb.

To commit is to give yourself to marriage without reservations. You can't say, "Well, if this doesn't work, I can get out," and expect a marriage to work. You can't say, "Well, I'll keep *that* marriage vow, but not the other."

Marriage is a long-term commitment. It precludes deep emotional relationships with other persons, specifically sexual ones. It is a declaration before witnesses that you are going to keep the awesome promises listed in the ceremony, that you will stand by through good times and bad, through sickness and health until death do you part. This is not to be taken lightly. It is why the legal contract must be preceded by some tough questioning of yourself and your partner.

There is no way to successfully fake this commitment. You can't say one thing and do another without paying a price. That people do so does not really mean they get by with it. They pay a psychic price (psychologists call it cognitive dissonance) if nothing else, or they reap a divorce.

Dove, Ostrich or Hawk, there is simply no way you can keep this legal contract without making a deep personal commitment to the marriage yourself.

Ten

Guidelines

No matter how lonely you feel after a divorce, or how in love you believe you are with someone new, marriage should not be considered until you have done some serious questioning both of yourself and your prospective partner. We have been so brainwashed by the concept of romantic love, and we are often so needy, that the thought of rationally evaluating the person we are about to marry seems almost un-American.

Even the most bruised and cynical will, when pressed, admit to dreaming about a good relationship, an ideal partner, one who would understand and fulfill his or her most secret needs for love and tenderness. It is fashionable to mock it, but idealizing is essential. If you have no ideal to strive toward, you will not be motivated to change or to risk yourself in another attempt to find what you want to make you happy. This is particularly true when you have been disappointed in your previous efforts.

That our ideal is too often unrealistic, too often drawn from marriages as portrayed in television films and stories, has been said again and again. Yet people go right on marrying—and divorcing. Statistics mean nothing when two people approach marriage. No one gets married believing the marriage will fail. Each couple *knows* they have something special going for them, and believe they are unique.

How do you know if you are *ready* to marry again? I have developed a set of guidelines that I believe will help you decide.

———◇———

GUIDELINE I—

Know Yourself

Know yourself as you are, not as you would like to believe you are or as you would like to be. (The self-unraveling questions and the quiz should help to give you a good picture.) You may be determined to make some changes and you will succeed to the extent that you sincerely put forth effort.

But be realistic. Change is gradual. Some traits are truly characterological. Others you may not want to change. They are you. In the first flush of love and in the sheer relief at the prospect of no longer being alone, you can convince yourself that you will be happy as long as you are with this new person. But you can't be with anyone all of the time. You are still an individual and you must come to terms with yourself to be happy or to make someone else happy. No one can do this for you or guarantee you a life without doubts or pain or disappointment, no matter how much he or she may wish to. If you find that you are too much of a Dove and it has hurt your previous relationships, recognizing it can be the first step toward change. But know, too, that this Dove response will be your immediate, automatic response to a stress situation and be prepared for it. The same principle applies if you are too much an Ostrich or Hawk.

Often we do not "see ourselves" because we do not want to. A woman with strong Hawk tendencies came to me in honest bewilderment after a second marriage failed. She bemoaned the fact that she could not look up to or respect either husband and utterly failed to see that she had totally dominated both of them. Nor could she acknowledge easily that both times she had carefully, if unconsciously, chosen men who *would* submit. She could not "see" her own behavior because she needed to think of herself as feminine as well as supremely rational. If she told others what to do, it was only because she was right. "I wanted them to take over, but they simply wouldn't. So I *had* to." Her compulsion to rule came from her fear of being pulled in a million directions, of going to pieces unless she kept herself under rigid control. She honestly believed she had to keep herself and everyone else on a tight leash or "something terrible would happen."

This kind of blindness is not as uncommon as it would seem. We can act a part so convincingly that the people most taken in are ourselves. It is easy to hide a need to control, for example, behind a great show of caring and concern and to mask hostility by being overprotective. Overfeeding when you have nothing else to give, or babying someone to keep him/her ineffectual and dependent are common examples of this.

Know yourself on a pragmatic level. If you require a certain standard of living, acknowledge it. Starving in a garret didn't work, even in *La Bohème.* If the person you love is not earning a great deal, be prepared to live moderately and to do without some things. Face the fact that physical attraction soon loses its freshness and that you will come to hate the living room furnished with Salvation Army "antiques" when you long for some solid comforts, not to mention luxuries. If you hate sports and your love loves them, you will be lonely unless you have an equally consuming interest. If you are a reader and the person you plan to marry was turned off books in primer days, you won't have much to talk about.

Above all, unless you know yourself you won't be able to make a sound judgment about anyone else. This seems to be one of those truths that you learn only by experience. When you are kidding yourself about you, nine chances out of ten you will kid yourself about the important person in your life. Falling in love has a galvanizing effect, but too often the effect is temporary. Over the long haul, it takes two real people to live in a real world.

---◇---

GUIDELINE II—

Know Your Potential Partner

We often unconsciously know more than we allow ourselves to admit about the people we marry. You may notice little things about the person you love during the courtship that bother you but you blank them. "That'll change when we're married"; "His last wife didn't understand him. That's why he's sometimes bitter about women, but he'll mellow with a real woman's love"; "He drank because he was so unhappy"; "She ran around because she had nothing at home"; "Her mother spoiled her; marriage will set her straight."

This is wishful thinking. We get fooled because we want to be or because unconsciously we *need* to be. Our perceptions are influenced by our needs, just as a table of food looks better to us if we are hungry than if we are not.

Whitewashing the flaws preserves the illusion that love can solve anything and you won't have to take yourself in hand. It's a good idea to observe your love with his/her friends and family and listen to their comments, even those made in humor. They may be trying to tell you something. If he/she keeps everyone, especially mother, hopping at home, he/she is probably going to expect the same service from you.

And listen to what is said about the *last* wife or husband or lover, particularly when it's negative. Are you sure it was all his/her fault? You could be next on the grill. "I wish I'd sat down and talked to his first wife. I'm sure she could have warned me," one woman told me. "He said she nagged all the time. Now everything he said she did, he says I do—and no wonder. He plays around all the time. He's never home." It would be cruel at this point to ask the woman what she expected. He was playing around with *her* during his last marriage. Did she imagine he would change?

Another sure clue to your new love's character is his/her behavior with waiters, waitresses, salesclerks, or anyone who is temporarily "serving" him/her. "No man is a hero to his valet" is a solid observation. People who are overbearing, rude or contemptuous when they can get by with it will inevitably turn that behavior on you when they feel safe enough to be themselves. I can't stress this enough. I've had so many clients tell me, "I should have known . . . he was horrible to waiters. Complaining and making them do things over. Well, that's a blueprint of the way he treats me. If only I'd been smart enough to spot it."

Again, it isn't that we aren't smart. This kind of blindness is not lack of intelligence, but allowing emotion to take over. You want him or her to be wonderful, the answer to a prayer—and presto—he/she is.

————◇————

GUIDELINE III—

Accept Yourself

Self-knowledge does not always mean self-acceptance. To *know* that you are ambitious, but to rail against it because it isn't "nice" or "feminine" means you have not come to terms with your ambition. Chances are you will try to repress that part of yourself you disapprove of, however fallacious your reasoning. And the part of you that you attempt to keep down will emerge, finally, in a big eruption, like divorce, or in a million small ones, such as unexplainable rages, headaches, depressions, martyrdom, misplaced energies, antisocial and self-destructive behavior. Like murder, the *self will out*, one way or another.

Conversely, if you are *not* something you are pretending to be because you know this is what the other person wants, you, and sometimes others, will also pay the consequences. Madeline, a Dove with almost no maternal feelings, had six children because her husband (who had doubts about his masculinity) wanted a large family. She was aware of her own feelings but thought they were unnatural, so she complied. She, her husband and unfortunately her children had to pay the price when finally she had a nervous breakdown.

In another instance a husband allowed his wife to have four children, although he was a deep-dyed Ostrich who hated domesticity and all of the problems that go with child rearing. He knew this about himself, but found these feelings "unacceptable." Again, believing he *should* like children, he convinced himself he did—for as long as he could. Then he simply walked out.

One woman I treated was incredibly curious, loved to travel, to explore new things. She convinced herself this was immature and that she should settle down and did—

into a bleak, joyless existence with a man who shared none of her interests or enthusiasms.

GUIDELINE IV—

Accept Your Partner

With self-acceptance comes acceptance of others—as they *are*, not as they will be after you have made some alterations. Marrying someone in order to change him/her rarely works. Even if you feel you are improving upon the original, your doctoring will be resented. For instance, if she is warm and loving, it would be nice but is it really necessary that she also be a gourmet cook, a perfect hostess, the most stunning woman at the party? If he is thoughtful and sensitive but likes to tie fishing flies and train hunting dogs, will it really improve your marriage to force him to go to literary teas and gallery openings? If his apartment was a mess before marriage, he is not going to become Mr. Clean by saying "I do," and if she was late for every date, don't expect her to meet your commuter train on time. There are always exceptions, but most kittens do not turn into lions, and probably the greatest thing to be said for being married is that there is then one person in the world with whom you can drop your armor and be accepted as you are.

GUIDELINE V—

Allow Time

Allow sufficient time after your divorce before you consider another marriage. You need time to adjust, to ask yourself what went wrong and how, and to re-evaluate your life and what you want. Rebound affairs and marriages seldom last. Consider yourself in a state of shock after any breakup, because emotionally, you are.

Allow significant time between consideration of marriage and the marriage itself. Give yourself a chance to know and evaluate your next partner realistically.

If you've married once, the statistics show that you'll probably marry again and that you'll stay married. Odds for success increase if a year or more has elapsed between the divorce and the second marriage. Statistics don't indicate whether these marriages endure for economic reasons, security, or fear of embarrassment over a second failure, but they do indicate that those second marriages that end in divorce do so in a much shorter period of time than do unsuccessful first marriages.

In my experience, a year between divorce and remarriage should be mandatory. Even more time is required if the person you are going with is also newly divorced. They may be *easy* candidates for matrimony, but not necessarily good ones.

———◇———

GUIDELINE VI—

Put Your Real Foot Forward

In your next relationship, put your real foot forward, not just your best one. And insofar as possible, encourage your new love to do the same. It is natural in the beginning to show yourself to the best advantage—to suppress the negative aspects of your personality. And of course, this works both ways: you are also seeing the other person in his or her most flattering light. And since you *want* to see your partner's best qualities, you often shut out nagging doubts. When something goes wrong it's natural to make excuses for the other person, and the ugliness of a quarrel can too easily be forgotten in the glow of making up.

Often this dual charade goes on far beyond the first meetings and sets the pattern of the relationship. One or both parties may know deep down that something is amiss, but each wants to remain a couple, to have a good relationship, so much so that they go on playing a role right into marriage, where the stress of everyday reality is bound to disclose the truth. Then disillusion sets in.

That our perception changes between courtship and marriage is so common it has elements of black humor. "He's so gentle and quiet" becomes "He's a bore. I can't get a word out of him."

"It's so nice to meet someone who is close to their family" becomes "She doesn't make a move without consulting her mother."

"He's such an individualist. Not caught up in all those false values" transforms to "He has no respect for anything or anybody and no manners."

"She's so alive and carefree—so much fun to be with" turns into "She hasn't got a thought in her head. I wish she would grow up."

"He's a fascinating talker. I could listen to him all night" becomes "He never stops talking. I can't get a word in. I wish he'd shut up occasionally."

"He's the casual type—a real man" turns into "I wish he'd dress up once in a while. He's such a slob."

It's obvious that if being the real you or seeing the real him or her is going to wreck the relationship, it is better that it happens before marriage than after. All of the people described earlier paid dearly for their illusions about themselves and the people they married, and all lived out a pattern imposed upon them earlier.

The split between *knowing* and *accepting* can probably

best be illustrated by heavy drinkers who may know they drink too much but don't really accept that it is a serious problem. They often marry believing they will change, convincing themselves that with a happy marriage they will be "saved." But of course they aren't, because they have missed an important step. You can't change unless you accept that you have a problem, long the tenent and probably one key to the success of Alcoholics Anonymous.

This principle of acceptance applies to changing any kind of behavior. You may recognize that you have behaved badly on an occasion. If you were severely punished as a child for any failings, however, you will often deny what you know to be the truth in order to ward off an onslaught of self-hate and self-punishment. Only when you can accept that you are sometimes envious or greedy or vicious, without punishing yourself unduly, can you begin to become *less* so in the future.

Imagine, for instance, that someone you care about has just had a great success in some undertaking and to your amazement and shame you find that your reactions are ambiguous. You are happy for him, but you are also envious of his good luck and find yourself mentally or actually saying something to cut him down. Instead of denying this feeling, or berating yourself, you could examine it—even talk openly about it. When brought to light, these feelings will evaporate or lose their importance in your mind. You are not a monster because you have envious thoughts. Perhaps you were feeling especially deprived that day. It is very likely that your friend had had similar feelings about you at various times. Suppressing "unacceptable" feelings actually makes them grow. Denying such feelings is taking another step away from being who you really are.

Accepting that we are often not what we wish to be is accepting our essential humanity, our fallibility. Only when we do this can we hope to grow.

Eleven

The Alternative — Remaining Single

Y OUR unraveling may have produced some surprises. You could well decide that you don't really want to marry again—for the time being or possibly ever. The prospect of making a formal commitment may be something you don't wish to undertake. This thought has probably occurred to you before, but you put it out of your mind. "It's not natural"; "What will people think?"; "There's something wrong with me"; "I must be too selfish . . . or too flighty . . . or too ambitious."

Now you can relax. You tried it once, so the pressure won't be quite so great. And you've grown up, so *you* can decide what you want. Freedom may be *the* priority for you.

You may really be happier unmarried. Many people are but won't admit it lest it sound like sour grapes. They cherish their autonomy and they're not afraid to be alone. This desire for solitude may, in fact, have led to the problems in their first marriage.

You may prefer short-term relationships. You may need variety and recognize that one person, no matter how attractive at first, will eventually bore you. You may need several people in your life. You may feel this way now and change later. You may feel this way permanently. It is *your* life and *your* decision. And today you can explore the possibilities of living alone, outside marriage, with less peer pressure and with greater freedom than ever before in history.

Since 1970 there has been a 134 percent increase in young adults living alone, and many recent newspaper articles have explored the phenomenon of our growing singles population. In recent *New York Times* articles it was reported how this dramatic shift from families to single adults has totally altered the economy and character of many large cities, and brought about a positive change in attitudes about the new single life style.

The increase in singles certainly had its beginnings with consciousness-raised, liberated women who demanded equal pay, equal opportunities to compete in the job market, and with changed feelings about marriage being the only goal worth striving for. Also, young women and men are leaving home at an earlier age to become self-supporting, thus creating an economically sound, growing population of young people living alone. Marriage may be part of their future plans, but first they want to learn about themselves, explore their capabilities, and possibly experience the new sexual freedom. Statistics show that in 1976, 56.2 percent of men and 45.3 percent of women under thirty-five years of age were single (never married), as compared to 50.7 percent and 37.6 percent, respectively, in 1960.

One woman who made a successful career as a lawyer after her first marriage was shattered told me, "I was going out regularly with Bill and we planned to be married, but suddenly I became 'Bill's girl' and soon I'd be 'Bill's wife,' and after all I'd gone through on my own, I couldn't take it. We still see each other . . . but I don't want to marry if 'I' have to disappear again and become an extension of someone else."

It is true that men face problems similar to those long faced by women, when they marry successful women. They can find themselves identified as "Helen's husband," and many men find this even harder to take than do women in parallel situations, with successful men.

There are other considerations. Would you be willing to leave the city to follow your husband or wife should his or her job require it? Honestly? A successful television actress I knew left New York when her husband was transferred to Philadelphia. Even worse for her, they moved out of the city because he wanted the life of an exurbanite. She hated it but endured for eight long (to her) years. When the marriage finally broke up, she had to start over again—eight years older and with her confidence at a low ebb. Had she allowed her real self a voice in the matter, she would have realized how much her work meant to her, that she was an actress by temperament and that she could never be happy in a quiet life out of the limelight. There are exceptions, of course, but they *are* the exceptions, not the rule.

The husband in the preceding case was not entirely straight with his wife either. During their courtship he seemed proud of her accomplishments and admiring of her talent. Yet the moment they were married he urged her to quit acting, even before geography made it a necessity.

Some people, usually Hawks, relish this kind of situation, seeing it as an exercise in power. They have to find out how much their partner is willing to give up for them. A CPA I treated had formerly been an English teacher, a profession he loved. But his wife, a Hawk, complained constantly about his low salary, and finally he gave up teaching to go into a profession he loathed.

Both of these people would have been better off remaining single—at least until they had developed enough of a sense of their own worth not to be taken over by another person. Deciding to remain unmarried, however, should not be an avoidance of assertiveness. It should be a conscious choice, a choice made with the same expectations for happiness and fulfillment with which people enter marriage.

"I love my new life," one new divorcee confided, "though I don't say much about it to my married friends. They would think I was only trying to cover my loneliness or pretending to be happy." What she enjoyed most, she said, was being able to read all night if she felt like it, or to get up at 2 A.M. and wander around the house and fix a sandwich or watch *The Late Show*, without having to explain her actions. She said she liked not having to fix dinner if she didn't feel like eating, not having to be cheerful in the morning, taking a vacation when and where she wanted and, she confessed, she liked having variety in her sex life.

She admitted that of course there were periods when she felt lonely, but the advantages of her single life far outweighed those moments. Actually, loneliness is very much part of the human condition, and is not necessarily erased by living with someone. Much of our attitude about loneliness is simply a product of our exposure to "ideal" love stories in all media. We are led to feel that togetherness is the *right* thing to want or aspire to, and that people who enjoy being alone are "weird," or at least "different." We are taught that loneliness is an "unmentionable," something never to be admitted, like a social disease. Because of this conditioning we are frightened of being alone.

Statistics indicate that singles don't do as well in terms of longevity, and that the suicide rate is higher among singles than among marrieds, particularly for men. This may say more about our societal attitudes than anything else. When people stop feeling that being alone is a reflection on their desirability and realize that they are perhaps the pioneers of a new and even enviable life style, these statistics may begin to change.

Once you have made the decision to remain single, or before you do, there are a whole new set of "rules" that can make it a rich and rewarding life. I have drawn these rules from the new "experts"—those who are single and like it.

1. Don't Camp Out

Try not to approach living alone as a form of camping out. In other words, don't think of this as a temporary arrangement until a new mate comes along.

Chris told me that even after two divorces and the determination never to marry again, she still wouldn't give herself "permission" to make her apartment a home—even though she had struggled for four years to extricate herself from her last marriage, move to the city, get the job she had dreamed of and establish herself *alone*.

"I've been in my apartment for three years now and it still isn't completely furnished. I never invite anyone to go there—I don't even like to be there much myself. I don't eat at home, there's never anything in the refrigerator. I keep forgetting to buy groceries. I guess if I did that for *me*, it would be an admission that I really am an adult now—grown up and able to take care of myself without a husband."

Chris was still treating her new life as a temporary arrangement, even though she had determined that marriage was not for her and that life on her own was worth striving for. She had made two beautiful homes, but they were for her husbands. She didn't know how to make a home just for herself.

2. Make a Home

Jeff, on the other hand, realized early on that he would probably never be able to marry. His personal freedom and privacy were dearly bought and paid for by the necessity to support aging parents until they died. By then he was well into his thirties. "I was in love several times, but I decided, when I got the chance, that I wanted to be *alone*. I wanted a home of my own with my own furniture in my own taste. I wanted to keep my own hours, entertain my own friends, choose my own vacations. You get that way after catering to two elderly people most of your life."

Jeff's home is a warm, happy place where people love to be invited. His dinners are famous, and he has more friends than anyone I know. These devoted friends include a number of former lovers. "My love affairs were all happy ones and we always parted friends." He is a truly adjusted single man.

3. Be Yourself

Another happy single lady chose her new life style after sixteen years of marriage. "I assumed that of course I *would* marry again, and this time I wanted a *real* man. Someone who would share decision making with me, and express opinions. Well, I found one and it's great! I can be as strong as I really am and he's not threatened by it. He likes me that way. But the crazy thing is, when he asked me to marry him, I found I didn't want that. I have a wonderful apartment that we both enjoy being in. We entertain a lot; we both have our jobs and everything seems so good, I can't see how it would be made better if we married."

Howard is another new single who finds that he likes being unmarried better. "I think I married because of pressure from family and friends, but marriage always made me feel constrained and boxed in. I hated feeling I had to check in and explain my actions. Now I ride my ten-speed bike to work (my ex-wife would have found a million reasons why I shouldn't); I've become a health-food addict and a good cook. I love the freedom to be who I am for the first time in my life."

Howard has women friends he sees regularly, but has no plans to remarry. "Marriage changes things, and women worry too much."

If you choose not to marry, or remarry, be prepared to treat yourself as well as you would treat someone you loved. Make your living space a "home" and you your favorite guest.

Twelve

Put Your Insights to Work

How do you know if your do-it-yourself unraveling has *worked*?

Let's assume you have taken the quiz, answered the self-unraveling questions and those pertaining to your marriage patterns. You have begun a ledger and you have learned to listen to your voices and make them work for you instead of against you. You have identified with some of the case histories and applied them to understanding your own experiences.

You have amassed an incredible amount of information about yourself and your last relationship. You have gained a great many insights into your behavior patterns and have begun to change them. You have some growing knowledge of yourself as you really are and of what you want to do with the rest of your life.

If your self-unraveling has worked, you will begin to make decisions based on the realities of your present situation, rather than acting out a pattern that may or may not be appropriate to your present life. You will have a stronger sense of self and of your own worth, of who you are and how you got that way, and some pride in your ability to survive and grow.

You will look at others with a new perspective, and they'll respond accordingly. They will not be seen as the "answer" to your loneliness. You are your own answer.

You will see your parents or the other important people in your early life realistically, neither condemning nor blaming, but accepting them as they were, not as they or you yourself would like to see them.

You will be able to react more spontaneously, and you will no longer be compelled to give in, to run away or to attack compulsively. You will be able to *choose* your response.

You will have made new friends, entered a new world, increased your knowledge and become involved in at least one meaningful activity outside your job.

You will know you can live through the anxiety that change and life problems engender, and come out stronger.

You will have a more realistic view of love and what marriage is and is not. You will know that you can live alone if you must—or want to. You will know what you need in a partner. You will know that you are in charge of your life, and though you might want to share your life with someone else, you don't *need* to. You will be sufficient unto yourself BEFORE YOU MARRY . . . Again.

About the Author

Dr. I. Ralph Hyatt is professor of psychology and chairman of the Psychology Department at St. Joseph's College in Philadelphia, as well as director of a counseling and therapy center. He was chief psychologist of the Pennsylvania State Correctional Institution and clinical psychologist for the Municipal Court of Philadelphia. He has written numerous articles for popular and trade periodicals and edited, with N. Rolnick, *Teaching the Mentally Handicapped Child*. Dr. Hyatt lives with his family in Philadelphia.